# FLORIDA GARDENING:

## the newcomer's survival manual

*by Monica Moran Brandies*

B.B. Mackey Books
Box 475
Wayne, PA   19087-0475

First Edition

FLORIDA GARDENING:  THE NEWCOMER'S SURVIVAL MANUAL

## DEDICATION

To my number one son Philip, his lovely wife Wanda, and sons Scott and David, buckeye and corn growers deeply rooted in the rich Iowa soil, as we were.  We differ in that Phil is just as happy when that soil is snow covered,  and likes it best when it is a pit of mud.
                                             - Monica Brandies

## ACKNOWLEDGEMENTS

Thanks to my publisher, editor, and illustrator Betty Mackey for encouraging me to do this book, to my family for living through my readjustment time, and to those who helped me relearn gardening in such a different climate:  to my friends in Rare Fruit Council International, to those I have interviewed for Tampa Tribune articles, to the people at the Hillsborough County Extension Service, to Vince Sims, to Gil Whitton who once answered my questions from Tampa to San Francisco and back, and to the other Florida garden writers whose books I have worn thin.

Books may be ordered by mail from B.B. Mackey Books, P.O. Box 475, Wayne, PA  19087-0475.  Titles available are:
1) *HERBS AND SPICES FOR FLORIDA GARDENS,* Monica Brandies, 1996 publication. $15.50
2) *FLORIDA GARDENING:  THE NEWCOMER'S SURVIVAL MANUAL,* Brandies.  $9.95
2) *A CUTTING GARDEN FOR FLORIDA*, Betty Mackey and Monica Brandies. $8.95.
4) *THE PLANT COLLECTOR'S NOTEBOOK*, Betty Mackey, blank journal for detailed garden notes on a plant collection.  $7.95
5) *GARDEN NOTES THROUGH THE YEARS.*  Four-year structured diary, for comparative notes on weather, bloom time, purchases, much more.$10.95.

Add $1.25 to defray shipping and handling.  Brochure mailed on request.
Wholesale terms.  Residents of Pennsylvania, please add 6 percent sales tax.

# CONTENTS

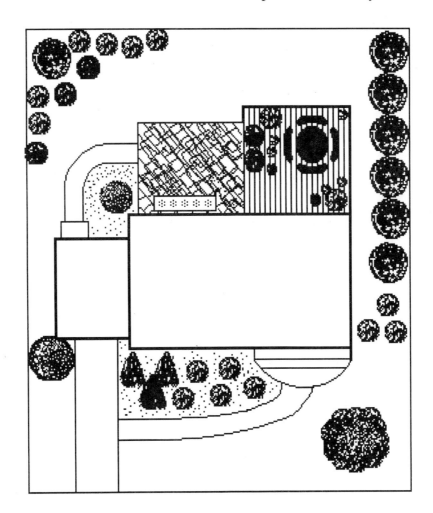

Site plan of a Florida yard

# CHAPTER ONE
# FIRST STEPS TO FLORIDA GROWING

You are about to move to Florida. Or maybe you just did. Or it still seems like you just did. What does it take to have a great garden?

Gardening in Florida is no harder than gardening elsewhere, but timing, techniques, plant selection, and insect control are different. When I moved from Iowa to Tampa, with forty years of gardening experience, I had to relearn gardening almost from scratch. Now, several years later, I am past the pain, but still learning. I understand the questions a new-to-Florida gardener will have. I hope that this little book will help you to a quick and successful adjustment to the delightful mystery of gardening in the subtropics.

## WONDERFUL WEATHER
If you are looking forward to pleasant, sunny days all year round, you will not be disappointed. Cloudy days are so infrequent that we transplanted people enjoy them as brief reminders of times back home. The same with cool days. Anything that involves frost is another matter which we will discuss later.

In any part of Florida, there are definite changes of seasons, sometimes subtle. Granted, the summer is hot, but most people have air conditioning and the use of their own or a neighborhood swimming pool. With these benefits, your first Florida summer may well be, as mine was, the most comfortable of your life.

It is not too hot to keep right on gardening, working for short spurts in the morning and evening through all the steamy months. And though some plants prefer cooler weather, many others will thrive. Because of the heat and humidity, fruit trees leap into growth and coleus cuttings root in a week.

## A YEAR-LONG GROWING SEASON
If you are a gardener, you will be looking forward to a year-round growing season.

During the steamy summer, you can grow heat-loving annuals like amaranthus, begonia, celosia, cleome, coleus, cosmos, crossandra, gomphrena, four o'clocks, impatiens,marigold, melampodium, narrow-leaved zinnias, ornamental peppers, portulaca, salvia of several types, torenia, vinca, and tithonia. Perennials like coreopsis, daisy bush, daylily, gaillardia, gazania, gerbera, shrimp plant, jacobinia, mallow, pentas, ruellia, and verbena do well. The vegetable garden may be on hold, but you can still pick okra, southern peas, sweet potatoes, cherry tomatoes, eggplant, peppers, and green papayas.

Summer is a great time to transplant trees and shrubs, prune a little, and gather and spread mulch. You can take cuttings to increase ground covers and many flowers, vines, and shrubs, for they root quickly with all the rain and humidity.

Then fall brings milder temperatures and a new beginning of the gardening season. Most flowers can be planted now. Sow seeds or buy plants. The ones that like cool weather, like alyssum, calendula, dianthus, pansies, petunias, poppies, snapdragon, and stocks, often will bloom in winter. Others seem to grow very slowly through the short days, but will be ready to burst into abundant bloom with the first sign of spring.

Most vegetables can go into the garden in fall, especially the ones that like cold weather, like cabbage, lettuce, carrots, onion, beets, celery, radishes, and swiss chard. You can plant strawberries and rhubarb, both of which grow as annuals here. Beans and corn may get nipped by frost, depending on where you live, but try some early plantings anyway. Now that it's fall, you'll start watering again, but it doesn't take too much water because the days are shorter and cooler.

Winter varies from nonexistent to short and sweet, depending on both location and year. Make the most of January and February (the closest we have to a dormant period) to do necessary pruning. Move plants when they are as close to dormant as possible if you are going to rearrange any of your landscaping. Keep planting seeds of flowers and vegetables so you can make the most of spring when it happens.

Water and feed plants as needed. Azaleas will need more water while in bloom. Their blossoms in midwinter are delightful, especially to your visiting relatives who will think that anything with green leaves is beautiful.

Spring sneaks up on you in Florida. But once you are sure there won't be any more frosts, there may be some garden cleaning to do. If anything seems dead, remember, it may come back from the roots. Cut it back but don't dig it up, yet.

You can grow almost any annual in Florida's spring. Azaleas finish their long season of bloom with a month of glorious color, and orange blossoms scent the air in March, my favorite month. You may start the season picking citrus, but before you know it you are picking peaches and plums in May. April and May come the closest to northern summer with their abundance of flowers and vegetables, but you have to water so much that you are ready for the summer rains to start.

## FLORIDA CLIMATE FACTORS

Florida has special conditions to keep in mind. It is, as one expert says, "a desert where it rains three months of the year." Because of the hot, humid summer, some plants cook out by July. So we treat many plants as annuals and start over with new plantings in September. Do this for most vegetables, even rhubarb, for many herbs, and for flowers such as petunias, snapdragons, calendulas, and pansies.

From September until the return of the summer rains the next June, many plants require irrigation to thrive, sometimes even to survive. And the number and intensity of frosts varies greatly from one year to the next.

We arrived in Florida in mid-June, just at the end of the growing season for most of the crops I then knew. That first summer was not the most encouraging, though even then it was much nicer than a northern winter. By the second summer, when the heat finished off my spring vegetables, I had fruit and ornamentals that jumped into such encouraging summer growth that the loss was more than balanced.

## TERRIBLE SOIL

Whatever soil you have worked with before, Florida's sandy, infertile type will be different. Longtime nurseryman Robert Perry says, "It holds the plant up. You have to do all the rest." That means fertilizing and watering more often because the soil retains little. In most cases, Florida soil is almost pure sand, though some areas have muck. Down below Miami and in the Key, there are about two inches of fairly good soil on top of Miami oolite, a porous limestone. Growers there must use an auger to drill holes in the rock before they plant trees. Any of these soils can and must be improved constantly with heaps of humus. Otherwise it is easy to work Florida's light soil.

Repeatedly adding organic matter is a good practice for gardeners anywhere. If you've already developed the habit, as I did years ago for Ohio clay, you are ahead. If not, you can develop both the habit and the enriched soil quickly by adding your own and some of your neighborhood's vast production of lawn clippings, leaves, and pine needles. Though I have been gathering mulching materials all my life, it has never been easier than here in Florida. In chapter 4 there are details about my methods.

## A BALANCE OF BUGS

You may hear horror stories about Florida's bugs. There are some whoppers, but then there are hardly any flies, so I'd say it all evens out. Your first big palmetto bug may cause your daughters to scream, but even they will get used to them and adapt. The mosquitoes are no worse than those in other places. You can garden here with no poisonous pesticides, or a bare minimum of them, if you wish.

We haven't had any spraying done by professionals inside or out in the five years we've been here, in spite of people saying we must. But that is largely because I personally prefer the bug I can see to the invisible poison that may permeate everything.

We are grateful for the arsenal of insect control measures, especially the increasing number of biological pesticides that do much less or no harm to the environment. I had been using *Bacillus thuringiensis* (*Bt*) before we moved and have needed it no more often in Florida. Mostly we just outlive the bugs as we did in the North. As with other aspects of gardening here, it's not more difficult, just different.

## THE NECESSITY OF NEW METHODS

If you are dreading the idea of learning all new gardening methods from scratch, this book is for you. When I moved from Iowa in June of 1987, I had been writing a weekly garden column for the local paper and a monthly feature for the Des Moines Register for some years. They promised to let me continue as long as I did not say things that would make Iowa readers envious. The first summer it was all I could do to conceal my own envy and depression. I felt like a fraud sending advice to northern gardeners while mint died in my yard.

I also kept thinking that I had been gardening for so many years up North and had still not learned all I wanted to know, so how could I ever live long enough to start all over. But take heart. Trees grow faster in Florida, and determined gardeners grow fast also, in knowledge and experience. Along with some failures, which gardens produce everywhere, there will be some wonderful successes right from the first.

There are several things you can do before, during, or after your move to ease the transplant shock and assure survival and quick new growth.

## ATTITUDE ADJUSTMENT

The most important thing to do is to adjust your attitude. Whether you've dreamed and saved for Florida living for years or had it suddenly thrust upon you by your own or your spouse's job, there will be certain misgivings.

During our last spring, I planted differently in the old yard. Instead of my usual experimenting, I concentrated on neatness and sure-to-succeed planting, two areas I tend to neglect, normally. Instead of a large vegetable garden, I planted flowers in masses of the same color to make a better impression on potential buyers.

Of course, you want to enjoy whatever you have in the old garden right up until you have to leave it. It would have been much easier to move in late fall because I don't miss winter at all. But the thought of never having lilacs and daffodils again seemed very sad at the time.

The fact is, there is now a family of hyacinth-flowered lilacs, with varieties like 'Blue Skies,' 'Lavender Lady,' and 'Silver King,' that is supposed to grow in Florida. And paperwhite narcissus grows out in the garden here. So will tulips if you give them cold treatment in your refrigerator. Once you get settled you'll realize that for every plant you give up, there are ten new ones to try.

Be aware, also, that some of the sorrow you naturally feel is transference. I couldn't bear to even think of the grown children and the little grandchildren I was leaving behind. I could express and control the idea of leaving the trees I had planted and nurtured.

The giving up of favorite plants, which was indeed painful, reminds me now of the priest who assured us that we could have anything we wanted once we got to heaven. We were school children at the time and wrote essays about the ball games we would always win and the pets we would have, and he assured us that we could have all that if we wanted it. "But when you were babies you wanted bottles and rattles, and now you couldn't care less about those things. And that is how it will be in heaven."

That is also how it will be in Florida once you adjust your attitude. You are going to love it so much that most of the things you no longer have won't matter. Children and grandchildren are obviously an exception. But there is no place people would rather visit, so friends and family you leave behind will not be lost to you.

## PACK OR TOSS DECISIONS

What you decide to bring along and what you give away will be greatly influenced by who is paying for the move and what you treasure most. It may be easier to discard garden items that you can cheaply and easily replace.

We have moved twice now at company expense. Both times I got rid of many things that I later wished I'd brought. I also discovered that single employees moved larger amounts than our big family, and no one objected. Don't discard things you want to keep unless you have to.

## PLANTS

Because the horticulture and citrus industries have so much at stake in Florida, there are laws that prohibit people from bringing plants into the state, unless they have them inspected at their departure point. If you want to bring plants, check with the agricultural extension service in your northern home several weeks before moving and follow their instructions.

Most moving companies will agree to transport plants growing in containers if asked to before the contract is signed, but will give no guarantee of their health or even life upon arrival. So I gave away the vast majority of my houseplants. I kept perhaps six most treasured.

The people who came to pack us kept saying, "None of these will survive. You might as well throw them away." So I gave away as many more as I could get the gathering crowd to take. But there were some, like the orchid, I did want to bring, so we piled them, with all the other forbidden things, inside the car that the movers were transporting. And in spite of a full week in the moving van in 90 degree weather, they came through just fine.

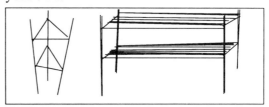

Many plants that grow as houseplants in the North are lovely landscape plants in much of Florida. From the Tampa area south there are fiddleleaf figs, schefflera, rubber plants, pothos, philodendron, and the like growing as trees, large bushes, or groundcovers outdoors. All of the common ones can be easily replaced, unless they were a Mother's day gift.

## SEEDS INSTEAD OF PLANTS

I collected plenty of seed, the ideal moving method for plants because it takes less space and undergoes no inspection. You can collect and label seed well before the move, and plant it well after. Once you get to Florida, store your seed in the freezer until planting time to protect its viability. Be careful to pack seed and garden supplies in well-marked boxes. I brought a trowel, spade, and hoe in the family's van and was digging for three days before the furniture arrived.

## EQUIPMENT

No mover questions the necessity of moving a lawnmower. My garden cart, composter, hoses, bird bath, porch swing, garden benches, statue of St. Francis, and a few other things made the movers mutter. But they were essential and I am glad I insisted. And if we had been paying for the move ourselves rather than through the company, I would still have moved those, even if I had to leave some furniture behind.

By the last morning of our Iowa packing we had reached the basement and yard. The movers spread across the front walk a great assortment of what they outspokenly considered junk. Much of it looked like junk. They wanted me to leave an old set of shelves that held canning jars. We had gotten it for free, moved it from Ohio, and would have to pay well over $100 to replace it. The same with my plastic compost bin, which I had washed out well. I finally bowed to the badgering and left my tomato rings behind, and it was 18 months before I found replacement wire that I didn't have to buy by the roll. Bear in mind not only the cost but the difficulty of replacing things in an area where you do not know the sources and where traffic may be too heavy for searching.

I gave away a pick-up truckload of canning jars and only brought the ones that were full. A family has to eat until a new garden gets growing. The movers who took us from Ohio to Iowa understood that but the Florida ones fussed a lot. If you get fussy packers or movers, ignore them. However, if you pack some of the smaller and more unsightly things yourself ahead of time and have the boxes sealed and labelled, this will save you explaining what non-gardeners can never understand.

You should pack any special flowerpots and planters, especially large ones, but don't bring more than a token few plain plastic pots. You'll be going to the nursery soon and you'll have more empties than you'll ever need.

Balance the cost of moving gardening equipment against the cost not only of replacing it but also the wear and tear of shopping, searching in vain, doing without, or going to a psychiatrist. You wouldn't throw away your child's favorite toys. Don't throw away all of your own.

## ALL THE INFORMATION YOU CAN GET

If you are getting ready to move, you have a thousand other details to worry about, so you may not even think of writing to the extension service for bulletins. Someone else had to give me the idea, but then it took only a few minutes to scratch out a letter to IFAS (Institute of Food and Agricultural Sciences), University of Florida, Gainesville, Florida 32611. If you have certain areas of special interest, such as trees, vegetables, lawns, flowers, fruit, or landscaping, mention them specifically.

Of course, you don't have much time to sit around reading, but you have to stop packing, or unpacking, and relax sometime. Reading about the exciting new plants you soon can grow and how best to go about it will restore your soul much better than TV will. The day my packet came from Gainesville, I cried with relief to read that I could still have dogwood trees. Iowa was too far north for mine to bloom except after the warmest winters. Tampa is on the southern edge of the dogwood's range, but the first March we were here the dogwoods were more beautiful than any I had seen since I went to college in Pennsylvania. They have not been as lovely since, but I haven't needed them as desperately.

It is because your time and energy are sorely taxed now that this book is small. It will help you bridge the gap. I am still relearning to garden in Florida. I have come far, but I still have the inexperience factor that is vital to the success of this book. Experts cannot imagine the dumb questions that we newcomers have, or the fears and uncertainties. After you get settled, you can buy from bookstores and garden centers or borrow from the library other books on Florida gardening. There are good newsletters, too.

IFAS can give you the address of your own county extension service. Find that building and stop in now and then to get free informational bulletins and ask the experts your most recent questions. Some extension sites also have demonstration gardens where you can observe or volunteer to help. If you have to live in an apartment for a time, this would be an excellent way to get your hands into a garden, meet other gardeners, and gain experience.

## HOPE TO KEEP YOU GOING

There will be times during the first year when you will be frustrated by failures. Bear in mind that this was true during any growing season farther north, but not to such an extent. But then, you never had a better excuse. Also keep in mind that your gardening is now in some confusion, along with, rather than in contrast to, the rest of life. It will all get better.

At first it seemed to me, especially in vegetable growing, that there was as much production and vigor as in the North, but it was spread out over twelve instead of, say, seven months, and never appeared to be as great. I still find this true for vegetables since they grow mostly in the cooler, shorter days of winter and only resemble northern production vaguely and briefly in May. Too many people give up because of that.

With trees, shrubs, and many flowers, growth has been so lush from the first that it more than makes up for problems in the vegetable garden. Keep trying and you soon will learn methods and plant varieties that ensure success.

Since later in that first year, my yard has looked as good, then better than any yard I had before. After five years, I have fruit, herbs, vegetables, and flowers to pick almost every day of the year. And the fruit is just beginning. My front yard looks great. In spite of seasonal weediness, the back yard is coming along well. I do not produce the 90 percent of our food that I once did (no cows or pigs here) but I do produce 75 percent of our fruits and vegetables. I know we will never go hungry. My workplace and my private park surround us. I am happy here, and it is a good place for my family.

---

### Newsletters and Magazines of Special Interest

**Living off the Land..** Marian Van Atta's subtropic newsletter that helps you live and garden better for less. Known best for information on warm-climate fruits. Look for the Van Atta's at meetings of rare fruit clubs. Send $14 for 5 issues per year, Sample issue $3. P.O. Box 2131, Melbourne, FL 32902-2131.

**Florida Market Bulletin.** Free on request, this delightful publication includes unusual sources for plants, seeds, and equipment. Ads for pick-your-own farms. Write and request it from Florida Dept. of Agriculture and Consumer Services, Mayo Bldg., Tallahassee, FL 32304.

**Florida Garden Guide.** Published by Lewis S. Maxwell, sponsored by Black Gold Compost Company. It covers things to do for two months, a planting guide, book reviews, and an illustrated article about some aspect of Florida gardening. Copies are free, from many garden centers, hardware stores, and extension offices. If you can't find it, send a stamped, self-addressed envelope to Lewis Maxwell, 6230 Travis Boulevard, Tampa, Florida 33610, for your nearest source.

**Florida Gardening Magazine.** Florida's Own Home Gardening Magazine. A new magazine, rich in Florida know-how and illustrated with color photos. Available on newsstands and by subscription (1 year is six issues for $16) to P.O. Box 500678, Malabar, FL 32950-9902.

**Southern Garden Gate.** This newspaper style publication is offered by subscription, and also free at some nurseries. It includes articles, a question and answer page, garden club activities, and TV and radio schedules of garden shows. One year subscriptions (6 issues) are available for $12 from P.O. Box 320954, Tampa, FL 33679.

**Palmetto.** The statewide publication of the Native Plant Society, mailed quarterly. It features information and description of Florida's native plants, some of which are underappreciated and worth more notice. This newsletter goes to all members; dues start at $20 a year. The state office at P.O. Box 680008, Orlando, FL 32868, will put you in touch with your nearest local branch. A membership will also bring you the local chapter's monthly or bimonthly newsletter. Guests are welcome at local meetings.

## FLORIDA GARDENING BOOKS

**The Book of Florida Gardening.** By Pasco Roberts, 104 pages covering soils, lawns, citrus, flowering trees and shrubs, month-by-month planting guide, and more. 1962. $3.95. Great Outdoors Publishing Company, 4747 28th St. N, St. Petersburg, FL 33714.

**The Complete Book of Edible Landscaping.** By Rosalind Creasy. Excellent description of how to use edibles and which plants are best for which zones. 379 pages. $14.95. 1982. Published by Sierra Club Books, San Francisco.

**A Cutting Garden for Florida.** By Betty Mackey and Monica Brandies. This 96-page book will introduce you to annuals, bulbs, perennials, flowering shrubs, and trees with which to fill your house with flowers. Month-by-month planting guide, bulb chart. 1992. Order from B.B. Mackey Books, Box 475, Wayne, PA 19087-0475.

**Growing and Using Exotic Foods.** By Marian Van Atta. Complete guide to growing fruits and vegetables in the subtropics. 180 pages. 1991. $16.95. Published by Pineapple Press, Inc. P.O. Box 16008, Sarasota, FL 34239.

**Florida Home Grown Series.** By Tom MacCubbin. Clear and practical advice from this popular public radio host: **Landscaping** (144 pages, $8.95), and **Edible Landscaping** (320 pages, $16.95). Published by Sentinel Communications, Orlando, FL 32801.

**Florida Landscaping Plants.** By J. V. Watkins and T. J. Sheehan. 412 pages. $13.95. Published by the University Presses of Florida, Gainesville.

**Florida Plant Selector, Florida Trees and Palms, Florida Lawns and Gardens, Florida Vegetables, Florida Insects, Florida Fruit, Florida Flowers,** and other titles. Widely available at local nurseries. Small, useful, inexpensive reference books, well illustrated. Published by Lewis S. Maxwell, 6230 Travis Boulevard, Tampa, FL 33610.

**Florida's Fabulous Flowers** and **Florida's Fabulous Trees.** By Winston Williams. Each is a full-color, beautifully photographed, 64-page guide to native and exotic plants that thrive in Florida. $9.95 each, published by World-Wide Publications.

**Flowering Trees for Central and South Florida Gardens.** By Maxine Fortune Schuetz. Beautifully illustrated with original paintings by the author. Gives requirements. 146 pages. $9.95. Published by Great Outdoors Publishing, St. Petersburg, FL.

**Garden Rebel Recipes.** By Robert Vincent Sims, a noted landscaper and radio host. His 32-page pamphlet includes home remedies for feeding, weed control, and pest control. $4.00 postpaid from Vince Sims, P. O. Box 1390, Mt. Dora, FL 32757.

**A Guide to Landscaping.** By Maxine Fortune. For professional planning, a plant selector for the tropics and subtropics. $3.95. 124 pages. Published in 1963 by Great Outdoors Publishing.

**Handbook of Florida Flowers.** By Lucille Proctor. This little book will help you identify, appreciate, and grow the flowering plants you see most often. $2.95. 48 pages. Published by Great Outdoors Publishing.

**Handbook of Florida Palms.** By Beth McGeachy. What palm is that? A great guide for only $2.95. 63 pages. Published by Great Outdoors Publishing.

**Living off the Land.** By Marian Van Atta. Pine & Palm Press. 1973. 64 pages of growing instructions and recipes for hot climate fruits, berries, and vegetables. Available from Marian Van Atta, P.O. Box 2131, Melbourne, FL 32902-2131

**The Southern Gardener's Book of Lists.** By Lois Trigg Chaplin. Lists the kinds and varieties of trees, perennials, ferns, annuals, vines, shrubs, and groundcovers that will do best and just how far south. 186 pages. 1994. $17.95, Taylor Publishing, 1550 W. Mockingbird Lane, Dallas, TX 75235.

**Taylor's Guide: The South.** Covers all, MD to FL. $18.95, paper, Houghton Mifflin. Widely available.

**Tropical Trees** and **Tropical Blossoms.** Two booklets by Bob and Dorothy Hargreaves. Each is 64 pages long, with 100 and 125 photos and descriptions. $3.50. Self published, available from Great Outdoors Publishing.

**Xeriscaping for Florida Homes.** By Monica Brandies. A resource for creating a colorful, efficient, beautiful, water-saving garden. Charts of grasses, groundcovers, shrubs, vines, and trees. 181 pages. $18.95. Great Outdoors Publishing, 1994.

**You can Grow Tropical Fruit Trees.** By Robert Mohlenbrock. Professor Mohlenbrock's excellent, illustrated guide. 80 pages. $3.95. Published in 1980 by Great Outdoors Publishing.

**Your Florida Garden.** By John V. Watkins and Herbert S. Wolfe. $12.95. Published in 1968 by the University Presses of Florida, Gainesville, FL.

**Wild Edibles: Identification for Living off the Land.** By Marian Van Atta. How to know, gather, and use over 25 wild plants found from Florida to British Columbia. 1985. 64 pages. $5.95. Published by Pine and Palm Press, P.O. Box 2131, Melbourne, FL 32902-2131.

* This is a sampling of resources available. Prices and availability are subject to change.

# CHAPTER TWO
## FLORIDA LANDSCAPING FEATURES

Florida, along with California, is leading the country into a new appreciation of landscaping. And why not, when we can enjoy outdoor living all year? A nice yard can make a great difference in life if it opens up outdoor living space for you and your family.

Here in Florida, because trees and plants grow year round, or nearly so, new houses can be surrounded with fast-maturing plants that look settled and lush in no time at all.

Many new residents are likely to accept whatever landscaping features come with the house and location they have selected. Yet changes are easily accomplished. Here are features to consider for future landscaping improvements or to keep in mind if you are still house shopping.

### SWIMMING POOLS

Many people who come to Florida do not consider buying a house without a pool. But, after seeing houses where the pool seemed to be most of the yard, even though surrounded by lovely shrubbery, we told our realtor not to show us any more houses with pools. About three days later we pulled into the drive of THE house that felt right and she said, "Oh, it has a pool, but it is above ground. You could get rid of it."

We looked anyway. We bought the house. The pool was only a fraction of a large, pie-shaped yard. We love both the yard and the pool. I like the above-ground pool for us because it is safer. Tiny children have to learn to climb before they can get in, and by then you can teach them to swim.

Our pool has a narrow deck and fence around the entrance half, and we've never had any child-in-the-pool scares. We do not have wildlife falling in and drowning, but our neighbors with in-ground pools do. If our pool is not perfectly clean it does not show, and if we ever want to get rid of it, we can easily. Also, it added much less to the price of the house.

Many yards with in-ground pools still have plenty of room for growing plants in other sections, and some of the best gardeners I know have pools.

An in-ground pools is often a lovely focal point for the house and yard, visible from the front door and most of the rooms. It certainly adds an air of luxury, but also quite a bit of upkeep. By the way, insist that your pool be sparkling clean and swimmable on your move-in day. You might be surprised at how expensive corrective treatment is, and what a delay in swimming the strong chemicals can cause.

Many Florida people live happily without pools. There are always neighbors who will share and community facilities.

### SCREENED-IN POOLS.

Many Floridians consider screened pool enclosures necessary to keep leaves and debris out of the pool, and to keep bugs out of the patio area. This has obvious advantages, but also some disadvantages to consider. The screen, especially on top, is prone to damage and difficult to repair. If you live near pine trees, the needles will stick into the screening and give it a furry look. Clean it out by spraying with the hose at high pressure

Screening cuts the sunlight falling on the pool area. The added shade shortens the swimming season somewhat, though it's good for growing plants under. We've had neighbors come use ours because it was warmer than their screened pools. Most native or settled Floridians only swim in their pools from about May to September. Pools are costly to heat and, as a rule, only hotel or community pools do so. I have swum in our unheated one in every month except January, but one must be set for fast-moving exercise (or crazy) to follow my example.

### GARDEN POOLS

Fishponds, water gardens, clear reflecting pools, fountains with trickling water: all were  once luxuries beyond the budget and knowledge of the average homeowner. With modern plastics, today's homeowners can put in a pool or fountain in one or two weekends at reasonable cost. A few evenings' study of water garden catalogs will tell you all you need to know. Maintenance is easier than you'd imagine, and winter freezing is not much of a problem.  Check building codes and consider safety.  Put your pool in the sun if you want waterlilies.

## HOT TUBS

Hot tubs are fairly common in Florida either as part of the pool, or as a separate unit, instead of or in addition to the pool.  The hot tub alone is less expensive and easier to install and fit into the landscape.  You can use it for a longer season than you would a pool because the water is heated.  It doesn't offer the exercise that a pool does, but it is even better for relaxation and also for therapy for many physical aches and pains like a bad back.  Florida hot tubs are often placed inside the screened-in patio or porch area to protect twilight and nighttime soakers from mosquitoes.

## BIRDBATHS AND FEEDERS

Though Florida birds do not depend on people for winter help as they do in the North, birdbaths and feeders are still attractive garden features that will pay dividends, bringing you interesting winged visitors who will help with bug control.  Put birdbaths where you can watch the birds use them.  Keep them clean and full, and you probably will see both familiar and unfamiliar species such as bluejay, meadowlark, cardinal, swallow, ibis, martin, and mocking bird.  Keep a bird book handy for identification.

## DECKS, PATIOS, SCREENED-IN PORCHES, AND SUNSHADES

Paved or screened outdoor living areas are common here.  Some houses have one or more of each type.

**Decks** are great for uneven yards or for houses that are above ground level.  The deck on its stilts can be level with the floor of your home.  You can build a deck into open air and have outdoor living without any steps.  You can also build it under the branches and around the trunks of trees for a natural roof and privacy without any harm to the tree.  You can build storage areas underneath some decks.  Florida decks often extend over water and combine with a pier.

A **patio**, screened or unscreened, may be more appropriate for a level area.  It can be paved with brick, stone, tile, or concrete.

A screened-in **porch** or **Florida room** is ideal because it is almost another room of the house for many months of the year.  It gives the best of both outdoor and indoor living.  We have

one and eat on it from April until October or later.  It is absolutely private.  It is great to sit where you can see out but not be seen, or reached by bugs.  I keep plants on our screened porch in winter to keep them from freezing.  Curtains of Virginia creeper and other vines shade it in summer.

Some screened-in rooms have windows as well as screens and are useful for all but the coldest periods, especially if they are on the south side, receiving heat from the sun.  Even during the coldest times, plants on such a porch will seldom freeze.

Some people prefer front porches from which they can hail their neighbors and visit with passersby.  Even if you are not so sociable, front yard structures can be useful.  We hope to put an arbor and patio by our front door.  Deciduous vines would then shade the front room from the intense summer sun, but would let in sun in winter.  A bench would provide a place to sit with Teresa, our youngest child, while she waits for the school bus, and for the older girls to sit and say good-night to their dates, and for me to set sacks of groceries while I unlock the door.  An overhead sunshade can make a big difference in air conditioning costs and indoor as well as outdoor comfort.

## OUTDOOR ROOMS

Try to make outdoor rooms an extension of indoor rooms:  a dining patio or deck with easy access to the kitchen,  an area for entertaining connected by French doors to the living or family room, a quiet balcony outside a bedroom.  Consider the sun, shade, and privacy created when you select and place your  plants.

Outdoor rooms need not be as well defined as indoor ones, but they need some of the same amenities:  something nice to look at, maybe walls, trellises, or hedges for a sense of enclosure, and a place to sit or have a picnic.  A solid surface for the floor is the first consideration.  Then comes seating.  If your outdoor room consists only of a bench, put mulch under it for convenience.  A bench on the grass is going to be in the way every time you mow.

## A MIRROR?

One couple with a long, narrow yard has a mirror hanging on one wall of their lath patio. It expands their view to include much of the yard that they could not see from their chairs otherwise. The mirror is so filled with the reflection of foliage that it blends right in.

## GARAGES AND CARPORTS

"We'll have to find a house with a garage whose door does not face the street," I told David when we were house hunting. We haven't seen or heard of any basements, so I could imagine what my garage would look like with the door open. We found a house whose garage had been exchanged for two rooms: a large study and a storage area. A carport had been added outside.

Carports are great because they hold a bicycle or two, but not enough junk to shame a person. They keep the rain and sun off your car and off you during your comings and goings. They shade the adjoining room and therefore save on air conditioning costs. Our neighbors were so impressed with the convenience of ours that they built a carport in addition to their garage. Ours is open, but theirs has decorative lattice on the sides. This might be restraining when loading or unloading, but it's very pretty.

## PRIVACY, HEDGES, AND FENCES

Our house came with a privacy fence surrounding the entire back yard. If it had not, I might hesitate to spend the money to install one. But I will not hesitate for a moment to say the privacy is wonderful. I can go out in my nightgown to feed the rabbits. I can make as many garden mistakes as I want and no one can see. I can swim without anyone seeing me in my bathing suit. Well, a few houses do look over the fence, but I trust they find us too dull for their entertainment. By the time the trees grow up, the privacy will be complete.

There are some disadvantages: cost for one, and upkeep for another. Cost can always be considered as part of property improvement. We have lived here over five years and have not had to do a thing to the fence. It is a natural gray

wood. I'm sure that we will have to pay for repairs eventually, but I will not complain.

I consider privacy the number one requirement for making a yard into an outdoor living space. It can be achieved instantly and at some expense with a fence or screen around the yard, around part of it, or only as a privacy screen between your own and a neighbor's patio or window. Fences do not seem to be considered as unfriendly in Florida, where they are quite common, as they were in the Midwest, where they were used only rarely. A fence gives a measure of privacy to the families on both sides.

A fence does mean that you may never meet neighbors in back that you might otherwise enjoy. In some cases, a partial fence or privacy screen may be preferable. It will also be less expensive. And that way the kids can still play a ballgame that covers more than one yard.

Plants too can provide privacy. Well chosen and situated shrubs, trees, or planter boxes are less expensive and can seem more friendly than fences. The plantings grow to maturity very quickly in Florida. Shrubs can grow six feet tall in only one to three years. In places where width is unwanted, select narrow or columnar ones.

Most people don't mind at all if the neighbors see them working, but would rather rest in some seclusion. So a green screen of shrubbery that is only chair height is still comforting. A raised bed or row of pots full of impatiens can do the job in color.

Many people plant formal hedges around their yards, and they are certainly effective for privacy. But constant clipping can be a hard chore. One neighbor's son gave his mother a hedge clipping for her birthday and worked for three days to get the job done. And in six months it needed trimming again. I would rather spend that time on other gardening chores. A clipped hedge is great, but be aware of the work you are getting yourself into if you choose to plant one.

## FOUNDATION PLANTINGS

We have to clip our pittosporum about twice a year to keep it from covering the windows and the front door. It was here when we came, and it is attractive, but I would rather have something that kept in bounds naturally. But so far, I have not been moved to dig it out and change it. Perhaps some day I will, and then I'll replace it with shrubs with edible fruit such as Surinam cherries.

Styles have changed, and foundation plantings no longer have to be moustaches all around a house. They can include small trees, open areas, edible plants, flower gardens, a bench or birdbath under a window, a basketball court by the garage, and almost anything else, as long as it harmonizes with the landscape, the house, and the people who live there.

## TURF

For many decades, grass has been used as a coverup for any spot nothing else claimed. No more. Common sense, shortages of energy (both human and fossil), and water shortages are turning grass into a design element instead. There is more about this in the lawn chapter. My spouse says I'd better cut our lawn down to size before all our children are too old to mow it. I use tons of mulch material collected in the neighborhood to surround trees, make new beds, and remove turf from areas for future plantings.

## FRONT YARDS

At one time, front yards were considered more formal and public than back and side areas. They were mown and groomed more for show than for enjoyment. That is no longer necesarily so. If the front yard has the best microclimate for fruit, go ahead and plant your fruit there instead of using the space for the same ornamentals that everyone else on the block is using.

Dooryards and entryways are spots that people see first and most often, so my most pampered flower garden borders the front walk. Why should flowers all be in the back where they don't show? They look great in Florida most or all of the year.

Service areas should be kept out of sight. Some subdivisions require clotheslines and vegetable gardens to be hidden from the street, or they forbid them outright. Check before you buy, if possible. By the way, vegetables can be cleverly mixed in with flowers and shrubs, or grown in containers, so that they are too attractive for anyone to notice or complain about.

One big shade tree was on the border of our front and side yard, so I immediately started a shade garden beneath its branches on the front side of the fence. It has looked pretty good from the first, and I am proud of it. On the back side of the fence are the rabbit cages, a shed, pots and potting soil, and an "intensive care unit" for plants I'm nursing along from seeds and cuttings. It is not as lovely. But it is private, and I have a bench in the midst of it, surrounded by ferns, where my visiting friend sits every morning to drink her coffee. She is the kind of friend who thinks rabbit cages are interesting. The neighbor children think the rabbits smell, but they seldom do: never do, to people used to Iowa hog farms.

## DRIVEWAYS AND PARKING AREAS

These service areas are often necessarily part of the front yard. Be sure to keep plantings low so as not to obstruct the view of cars entering or leaving. Make driveways wide. If there is room, a circular drive will eliminate the need for backing into traffic. So will an L- or T-shaped turnaround area that can double as a play area or entryway. If you do not want to have all of this in hard surface, consider an area of bark or woodchip mulch for turning around or parking extra cars out of the way.

## GARDEN PATHS AND WALKWAYS

Paths provide access that opens up a yard. Have you ever watched a small child try walking on grass after a long winter of learning to walk on solid floors? That soft, oddly textured, sometimes dewy surface goes against the grain. Our feet like to follow a path with a predictable surface and direction.

Hard paving, cement, brick, or stone, usually leads people from the street or sidewalk to your front door and from the parking space to the back entrance. Other paths from the rest of the yard also lead to these areas. Side paths can be stepping stones, pine needle, pebble, bark chip, or wood chip mulch, or anything else that will keep the feet dry and set out the direction.

Part of adjusting to a new garden involves planting certain plants that you want to see or pick often, in places where you can reach them easily. Parts of the garden that require early morning access should have paths with a solid or at least a mulched surface. Grass walkways may suffice for getting to distant areas after the dew dries off.

Some portions of most yards are doomed to neglect by their distance from or lack of connection with anything important. We no longer have our pool on an automatic timer, so someone has to walk to the pump morning and night to plug in or unplug the motor. Any plant along this well-traveled path is sure of attention. Plants out by the shed may only be noticed when someone gets out the lawnmower. Since that is usually an otherwise non-gardening teenager or Dad, those plants still get no attention. Any plant near the back or front door or the mailbox is sure of constant notice and care.

The principles of xeriscaping (gardening with a minimum of irrigation) come into play here. Plants that need frequent watering should be grouped together as near where the hose turns on as possible. Plants that need only occasional watering can be at the far reaches of the hose. Those that are native and will survive on natural rainfall can go as far out as you like. But even those will need water for several weeks or months when they are newly planted.

Paths should flow with the natural route of traffic. Curves and crossways should have a purpose. If a path meanders around without a good reason, just watch how children or even your own feet will make a new one to get more directly where you want to go. If foot traffic wears paths in your lawn, add paving where the need for it has been so clearly shown.

Plantings and walls near walkways should be low and far enough from the walk that they do not crowd it. Make paths wide enough for carrying groceries, wheeling a garden cart, or whatever use you foresee for it in the future.

## MULCHING MATERIALS

Weed growth in Florida is no more insidious than in any other place I've gardened. But the grasses are especially tough and rampant. On his first visit to us, our grown son Mike laid out a path to the pool with paving blocks set in a bed of sand. Within a year, the path was entirely lost in encroaching grass. David dug out the blocks, removed the weeds and grass from the area, put black woven mulching cloth underneath the sand and black plastic edging along the sides, and reset the paving stones. He still uses a little Round-Up (TM) along the sides as needed, but the path has been clear and clean for several years now.

The previous owners put in a sandbox play area larger than the living room, and surrounded it with railroad ties. We wish they had used mulching cloth under the sand, because grass grows right through, and we can never keep it clear. The neighbors have a similar problem in a bark-mulched area in front of their house. It looks nice, but the weeds are constantly creeping through. Mulching cloth would prevent most of these weeds.

## LIGHTS FOR OUTDOOR LIVING

Garden lighting is a new trend that is gaining favor because low-voltage systems are not too expensive to buy or use, and easy enough for even an unhandy person to install. There are even solar-powered lights with no wires to worry about. Lights offer security as well as extra enjoyment of the garden. With them, you can work, eat, entertain, or walk in the yard and

## MULCH MATERIALS

| KIND | AVAILABILITY | COMMENTS |
|---|---|---|
| grass clippings (see page 24) | free, plentiful | beware of herbicides |
| leaves | free, plentiful | look better if shredded in leaf grinder |
| wood chips, bark chips | can cost | call utilities, tree trimmers |
| pine needles | free, plentiful in certain neighborhoods | attractive |
| newspapers black plastic mulching cloth | free inexpensive worth the price | put these under other mulches to make them more effective |

garden through the long dark evenings of winter as well as the twilight ones of summer. Lights allow you to accent the good points of a garden or dramatize architectural features. Less attractive parts of the yard add mystery by being in the shadow. Even if the weather is bad and no one goes out, lighted views or pool lights shining beyond the large windows or glass doors give added elegance.

I just put in my first set of lights, and suggest using a kit for starters. It is more fun than Christmas. Son Tom helped me figure out how one set of six tier and four floodlights could light three front gardens. My plan for the next set includes that path to that pool motor plug we too often forget until after dark.

## STORAGE AREAS

Garden sheds can be as attractive as they are handy. Situate them for convenience, add racks and hanging space, shelves, a potting bench, and a place for pot and garden product storage. Lath siding, windowboxes, or other design features that harmonize with the house and landscape help them blend in. One of the sheds we inherited lacks a door. To screen the unattractive entrance, we put up a section of crisscross lath to support a flowering vine.

## EDIBLE LANDSCAPING

This idea is such a natural for Florida yards that I can hardly believe how few people consider it. It must be the farmer in me that still says, "Plant something you can eat." The same plants can be beautiful, and are certainly more interesting than the privet hedges, azalea bushes, and hibiscus shrubs that you see in every yard.

Plant the edibles just as you would any other ornamental plants. Among edible plants are annuals, perennials, shrubs, vines, and trees. Keep in mind all the features of the plants you choose. How large will they be? Will they give shade or privacy? How will they look and smell in flower and fruit? Can fruit drop without mess on mulch or grass, rather than staining the driveway or patio? Are the plants likely to suffer frost damage or have other times of looking less than lovely? If so, for how long and for how often?

Chapters 5 through 10 discuss the individual edible or ornamental plants in detail.

Most of us want ornamental plants as well as fruits, herbs, and vegetables. And there are some people who don't want dropping fruit anywhere, and pay extra for fruitless mulberries and such. But for those of us who have genes that remember past famines, and don't mind a little extra chopping in the kitchen, edible plants are preferred. A dual purpose tree, shrub, groundcover, or flower is what we look for first, before our growing space is all used up.

# CHAPTER THREE
## EVOLVING YOUR NEW LANDSCAPE PLAN

Some friends of ours moved to their new Florida house and put in a swimming pool in less time than it took me to put up my clothesline. They knew right where they wanted it and have never been sorry. They never found a place where it would get more sun or fewer leaves blowing in, or where it would be more convenient for access to the kitchen or the bathroom.

But for most people most of the time, it is a better idea to live in a new house and its surrounding grounds for at least a year before making any big decision or doing any expensive landscaping. During your first year your landscaping plan can evolve. After the first cycle of seasons, you will be ready to finalize your plan. From then on, it will help guide you to your ideal yard for indoor-outdoor living.

This evolution is even more important with such a change in climate, plant material and methods as newcomers to Florida face. And the final plan is also more important in Florida than in the North because here there is so much more opportunity for year-round enjoyment of the outdoors.

A good landscaping plan is like a road map. With it you will not waste work time or growing seasons, money, or energy in the months and years ahead. However, you will go on learning, so even the best original plan will require minor alterations from time to time.

### DON'T WAIT FOR SHADE

Shade trees are the exception to the waiting rule. If you don't have any or enough shade, plant one or two trees, the largest size you can afford, as soon as possible. Don't plant them too close to buildings, a common mistake. (That rule goes for seedlings of large trees as well.) Study reference books and mature specimens and visualize that tree full grown. Put it where the canopy of branches will shade the house but not threaten it.

### WHICH TREES SHOULD I PLANT?

Your local nurseryman or extension agent can recommend several kinds of trees from which to choose. From central Florida north, oaks are excellent. Laurel and live oaks are evergreen and are strong wooded although they can grow as much as five feet a year. Pin oaks turn a brilliant red in the winter, giving a northern feeling. The colder it is, the more brilliant the color. Holly trees do not spread as far but are lovely in leaf and berry. East Palatka and Savannah hollies are most often recommended. By the way, only female holly trees bear the red berries (fruits), and only if pollinated by a male tree. So plant one of each, or several females and one male. If space is tight, you can plant a male and a female in the same hole. Slash pines can be planted in clumps for shade. Many people enjoy magnolia or camphor trees. Poincianas bloom yellow and red in the summer; golden rain trees in September.

Trees grow much more quickly here. Landscapers also can now move very large trees, as you will see if you watch new industrial properties. Until your trees grow, use vines for instant shade, color, and privacy. See much more on vines, trees, and ornamentals in chapter 9.

*Consider these landscape factors:*

*What do you and your family want from your yard?*
*How much time and effort do you want to spend?*
*What areas are most easily seen from indoors looking out?*
*Where do your shadows fall, and when?*
*How much privacy do you want? Where is it most needed?*
*Do you want to keep every tree and shrub?*
*Before you remove it, what does it do? When?*
*When this baby tree is matue, where will it spread?*
*What are the best places for trees, gardens, patios, and paths?*
*Can service areas be made inconspicuous? Joined together?*
*Is there a nice vista to emphasize, or an eyesore to hide?*
*Where do you want to start? Which sections which year?*

### WHAT IS THAT TREE (FLOWER, SHRUB, VINE) I SAW?

As a gardening newcomer, you'll probably ask this question frequently. You will learn many of the most common plants within the first year if you keep asking and studying. But the rest will take a lifetime, just as they did in the North. Don't stop asking questions. You'll soon find out who has the answers and who doesn't.

Go to visit public gardens (see the list in the appendix) where trees are labeled. A season ticket to Cypress Gardens cost me only ten dollars more than one for the day, so I went as often as I could with camera and notebook to see what was blooming, dormant, or promising. The public gardens nearest your house are not only the most convenient for this, but also the most useful. Hardiness and behavior of plants can vary in surprisingly few miles.

Look closely at the landscaping in your own neighborhood. What looks good? How big is it? What needs too much care? This will help show you what the plants will do in your yard.

Some local cemeteries also serve as arboreta. One in Tampa puts out a brochure describing the special trees you can see there. I went just to see what a monkey puzzle tree would look like at maturity before I planted my small one. It turned out that there was one right up the street and several more in my neighborhood. But I didn't know that until my visit.

### PRECAUTIONS WHEN BUILDING

If you are building on a new lot, it is a law in cities like Tampa that you call in the forestry department. They will help determine which trees are choice and should be saved even if you have to change your house plans, and which ones you can remove without any qualms. This is a most valuable service, and where it is not furnished by a goverment agency it would be well worth the cost to call in a tree expert to evaluate your trees. Otherwise you might remove something irreplaceable.

During construction, protect the trees you want to save from contact with the building machinery and also from soil compaction. If you must change the grade more than a few inches, build a well or terrace several feet away from and surrounding the trunk, and bank it with stone or railroad ties. Otherwise the smothering or scraping of the root system could slowly kill the tree. City forestry departments gladly make suggestions in such cases and often manage to save prize trees in the most difficult situations.

### WHAT ABOUT WHAT I HAVE?

If feasible, ask the former owners to write down the names of all the permanent plants in your new yard. That will save you digging up or planting over something special.

Florida is one of the few places I've seen where so many yards have too much shade. This is fine for keeping the house cool, but can be a drawback if it makes the house dark and gloomy or if you want to plant fruits and vegetables or sunloving flowers. To get more light and air circulation, and perhaps a better view, prune trees to have higher crowns and fewer low branches.

Eventually, you may want to remove less choice trees or shrubs, but don't remove anything until an expert recommends it or you live with it in every season. And even then, be very conservative. If you move in after a bad winter, some of what you see can be misleading. A tree that is usually beautiful may have skipped that year's bloom.

Start a garden notebook and record plant names, locations, and bloom times. Keep records on those in your own yard and also those of interest from other places. This will be a good base for future plans.

### WHEN CAN I START PLANTING AND USING THE YARD?

The day you arrive, you can start planting if you want. Hands-on experience is the best teacher. But at first plant only annual vegetables or flowers or small plants that you can move. Plant where success seems most likely. Experiment. Be prepared to change plantings when you are more familiar with your yard and its microclimates. Make use of containers (see chapter 10), for they are portable. When you get a four-pack of plants, put some in one location, some in another, and compare the results.

Florida lawns, unlike those in colder states, can be started almost any time of year, as long as they receive plenty of water. For details, see chapter 5. In most of the state, soil is so sandy that mud is not a problem around new homes.

You will want to start enjoying the outdoors right after your move, for outdoor eating, visiting, sitting, and play. Young children will soon find or make their own play areas. Try to guide little ones to or situate swings and play equipment within easy view of where you will be working or sitting. Go ahead and wear down the grass as needed in such areas, and for garden paths. Later, you may use these spots as a guide in situating decking and paving. You can make temporary paths and patios with a mulch of leaves and pine needles or small bark chips.

If you want a deck right away but are not sure where to put it, build a temporary one in sections that can be moved later if necessary, or incorporated into the permanent finished deck.

## FLORIDA GARDEN FACTORS TO CONSIDER

* **Shorter days.** In Florida, during fall and winter, day length gradually decreases by up to three hours, and the sun is lower in the sky than in summer. Most garden plants are sensitive to this and grow faster when days are longer. Although the decrease in day length is not as pronounced as it is farther north, it happens during Florida's main growing season. Growth of flowers and vegetables in winter seems slow to gardeners from cold climates where summer days are very long. However, the long Southern growing season more than compensates for it.

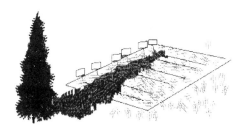

* **Sun and shade.** The amount of sun or shade a garden spot receives varies greatly with the seasons. Because of the changing angle from which the rays fall, many plots in the yard will be too shady for a fall or winter garden. The same plots may not see so much as a shadow all summer. This came home to me very clearly when my son moved down in the spring and put a dog pen in the yard. The dogs nearly perished from the heat. When the pen was moved by fall and I thought to plant vegetables there, I found, to my surprise, that there was not enough sun.

Because trees grow much more quickly in Florida, shade soon closes in beneath them. One plot that was ideal in our first few winters is already too shady for most vegetable crops. Also bear in mind that many plants, like beans, need all the sun they can get to grow well in fall and winter, but another location with some shade will keep the same plant growing a few weeks farther into the summer.

* **Feeding** is a must. In Iowa I grew many crops with no fertilizer at all. Only weeds will grow without feeding here. Along with the organic matter, spread some all-purpose fertilizer like 6-6-6 with trace elements included just before planting. Then feed all crops again when they are about two inches tall and again when they bloom. Spread about five pounds to a 50 foot row or 50 square feet every time.

It is easier to bring home, and spread the much smaller recommended amounts of slow-release fertilizer, though it is expensive to buy. I find a 50-pound bag of Osmocote (TM) will last a year or more for our entire half acre yard and it is well worth the price (around $50). Usually, one application of this will carry a crop of vegetables or annuals clear through the growing season, but if they begin to show pale leaves, add more.

* **Water,** so abundant in the summer, must be supplied by some type of irrigation the rest of the year. Most of the vegetable growing and much of the flower growing is done in the dry season. An automatic irrigation system is ideal, but this must be adjusted to the season. Your garden needs less water in December, when it is growing slowly, than it does in May when growth is lush and fast.

The first year here I laid out a drip irrigation system with paperlike tubes. The project was neither too difficult nor too expensive, and worked very well without wasting any water. Unfortunately, the fragile system perished in the replanting. I recommend it for the careful grower and for permanent plantings. Permanent drip irrigation systems are highly recommended for all areas.

One friend bought a house with automatic sprinklers for the front lawn but none in the back where she did most of her gardening. If I ever install sprinklers, it will be in the opposite order, back first, front later. Meanwhile I get along all right with plenty of hoses to reach all areas, some soaker hoses for special spots, and portable sprinklers. Of the latter, the longest lasting and most effective so far has been one that sprays with a revolving circle at the top of a three-foot stem. I can easily move this from plot to plot. Until I find something better for me and my budget, I am planting flower and vegetable beds where the water falls from each move of the sprinkler.

* **Salt tolerance** is of no concern to inland homeowners, but is top-of-the list concern to people who live on the coast or on coastal water-ways. Many plants, like sea grape, oleander, Jerusalem thorn trees (Parkinsonia), magnolia, jasmine, gaillardia, palms, live oaks, yucca, and natal plum tolerate salt spray very well. Others, like citrus and bottlebrush, have fair tolerance. Bamboo, gardenia, and croton have poor tolerance. And bird of paradise, dracaena, caladium, orchids, spathiphyllum, banana, ginger, hibiscus, and figs have none. If you live on the seaside, ask your nurseryman or estension agent or check with the Maxwell or Watkins book (see page 10). Some of Florida's loveliest yards are on the water, and it is not impossible or difficult to garden there.

Bette Smith, who writes the garden page for the *St. Petersburg Times* and has one of those delightful yards on the edge of Treasure Island, tells us that man-made soils like hers are very alkaline. She uses chipped sulfur in a whirlybird thrower to keep the pH down to a workable level. Two treatments a week apart can last for years, she says.

* **Insects** are never frozen, seldom even chilled here (see page 6), so bug patrol is very important. If you don't find the tomato horn-worm soon after it appears, the tomato leaves disappear. Some say a whole privet hedge can disappear. On the other hand, when I see the striped larvae of the swallowtail or monarch butterfly eating away at the butterfly weed, I let them eat. So far they seem to progress to their next stage before all the plants are denuded and their pruning isbeneficial.

* **Snakes** exist in Florida and a few of them are dangerous. But I'll be darned if I let that keep me from gardening. I often announce my presence; "Okay, snakes, get out of here. It's my turn in the garden."

If I lift a log or other logical snake hide-away, I stand back with a hoe handy. But I get rid of likely hiding places and don't worry about snakes. We seldom see any and only once saw a poisonous one. One friend of mine refused to even go for a walk for fear of snakes, but we are much safer working in the garden than driving on the roads, and we take that in stride.

* **Bees** can be scarce in Florida. Although there are hives nearby, there is so much bloom-ing that the bees do not need to fly the two miles they did in Iowa. I had to hand pollinate the squash and plant the bees' favorite plants (butterfly weed, bottlebrush bush, lavender, etc.) for two years before many came around and there still are not enough. All the development has reduced the wild bee population. Consider having a local beekeeper keep some hives in your garden if necessary.

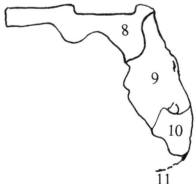

* **Zones of hardiness.**. I always checked the USDA hardiness zones to see how much cold a plant would stand (eg. hardy to Zone 3) before I moved to Florida. Now I look for a range of hardiness zones (eg. hardy from Zones 6 to 10).

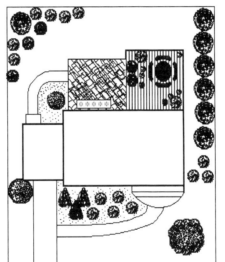

Most of northern Florida and the western panhandle are in Zone 8. The southern quarter of the peninsula is in Zone 10 and some of the Keys in Zone 11. Tampa is smack in the middle of Zone 9, according to the zone map, but I still find that many plants recommended for "Zones 3 to 9" will not grow here or grow only in certain seasons or with special care. That's because our part of Zone 9 is hotter and more humid in summer than some Zone 9 Western US areas. The USDA Zones are based on minimum, not maximum, temperatures. Nevertheless, those plants I really want are worth trying. If a plant isrecommended only for Zones 2 to 8, it will probably resent the heat and humidity, even in Zone 8. If someone gives you a plant, try it and see what happens. Plants are unpredictable, and you might be lucky. Just remember that summer heat can be as important as winter cold. Naturally I now favor catalogs like Park Seed, Thompson and Morgan, Hastings, and Wayside Gardens that indicate both cold and warm zonal limits.

* **Translation** of all garden information becomes important. Even this book contains advice that must be adjusted to different parts of the state. When you can, choose books that give both the northern and southern zone limit for each plant. Any garden book that does not talk about the effect of heat and humidity on plants will not be very helpful to Floridians. Some great ideas work anywhere. Others need a bit of adjustment for each climate. And some ideas that you read in general garden books won't work in Florida at all.

For your first year in Florida, you may want to let most of your reading come from the list of books in chapter 1. But don't cancel any catalogs or magazine subscriptions or throw away your garden reference books. At first you may feel leery of former sources, but soon you'll be able to interpret them for Florida gardening. Past experience does not disappear. Don't bury it, just rearrange it to suit present needs.

* **Local conditions** take on added importance. Florida gardeners will get the most appropriate plants as well as advice from local nurserymen or southern sources, although some plants from California are also adaptable. Only some or certain varieties of the plants from general catalogs will do well here.

Also take all new advice with a grain of common sense. One man whose terrific vegetable garden made me stop to meet him told me that I could not grow English peas here. I can and do, although we never get northern-size harvests. The secret is planting in November. A girl at my favorite garden center told me never to use peat moss or potting soil in the ground. I can't imagine now why not. Peat moss is one of the best soil amendments here because it lasts much longer than the fast-disappearing compost and retains water and nutrients so well.

But most of the advice I've gotten has proved true. I always did garden against some of the rules, planting extra late or early, or growing borderline plants. I was determined to continue this in Florida, but I found that it is much harder, and often impossible, to go against the rules of timing and seasons. Here again, it is best to learn and obey the rules first. Then later you can break them with better discretion.

**DRAWING UP THE ACTUAL PLAN**

As you learn Florida plants and growing methods, you will automatically begin to evolve a landscaping plan, at first only in your head. Don't let it stop there. Get it down on paper, even if only in sketchy form. Use copies of any deed or lot diagrams that came with the deed to draw your plan to scale. Graph paper works well and you can let each block represent 1, 5, or 10 feet. Getting your yard on paper will open your eyes to dimensions you may never otherwise realize. If you have no diagram, measure your yard with a tape measure or by pacing off the outer borders, the distance of the house corners from the property line, the placement of trees, pool, driveway, and other permanent features.

You can then lay tracing paper over the base plan and experiment with different arrangements. Or cut out scale drawings of desired improvements like gardens, patios, paths, and such, and move them around until you have an arrangement that suits you. Garden writer Ellen Henke likes to cut out flowers from seed catalogs and play around with combinations of colors and textures until she achieves the desired effect for her plan.

## DON'T FORGET THE VIEWS

Much landscaping, even in Florida, should be done from the inside looking out. Give every window a pleasant view and let most garden improvements be situated for enjoyment from the inside. Frame and preserve the pleasant views that are already there, including your neighbor's lovely tree. Be careful not to plant anything that will block your view of the flag on the mailbox or the coming school bus. But plant something beautiful to cover or draw the eye from your own or your neighbor's garbage cans or compost pile or clothesline.

## PLAN FOR COMMON SENSE MAINTENANCE, PLUS XERISCAPING

Include only the planting you reasonably expect to have time to maintain. I love my large yard, but many people would hate it for causing too much yardwork. And even I am working to eliminate much of the open grass area with mulch and woody plantings. This will save mowing and watering.

In this day of environmental concern, and in this state of frequent water restrictions, it is important to plan your yard according to the principles of xeriscaping (drought-tolerant landscaping) for beauty and success in plant growth, for lower water bills, and for commonsense care of the environment.

Besides employing soil care principles which help the soil hold water better (discussed in the next chapter), xeriscaping means grouping plants according to their water needs, with the thirstiest ones usually closest to the house, the ones that need only occasional watering once established in the next zones, and native plants that will survive on natural rainfall in the rest of the yard, indeed in most of the yard if you are looking mainly for low maintenance.

Another principle involves reducing turf area. Instead use large areas of mulch and/or ground cover, especially beneath trees. Use turf as a design element, not as a coverall, for lawn takes more work, more water, and more fertilizer and pesticide than any other part of the yard, especially in Florida where you have to mow at least weekly all summer and less often, but still occasionally, the rest of the year.

If you plan to undertake extensive changes, the services of a professional landscape designer or architect will be most helpful. However, take time first to familiarize yourself with Florida plant possibilities, and make your preferences and ultimate goals regarding use of the space clear. Try to see examples of the work of several designers before making your choice.

# CHAPTER FOUR
## DIGGING INTO A NEW YARD

I started digging and planting in my yard while the rest of the family were still enjoying motel living. The work produced little plant growth, but it made me feel better. It was difficult to break the sod, but where no grass was growing, digging was as easy as in a sand-pile. Our yard is pretty much one big sandpile. And even I had not packed compost in the van.

Getting organic matter such as compost into the soil is the first essential rule of Florida gardening. If you bring or buy plants, leave them in their containers for the time being. You can move them when you see where the light is best and rearrange your landscaping as you learn what the plants are going to do where.

### CHOOSING GARDEN SITES

Each kind of plant has its own preference for soil type and amount of sunshine. However, few plants grow in soil as infertile as that in much of Florida, so plan on improving any site on your property.

The spots you select for fruit trees should have as much sun as possible. Vegetables and many flowers should be in full sun or light shade. Full sun is best from September to May. Many plants that loved sun in the North will thank you for some shade during the summer months in Florida, and some will die out without summer shade, even if your seed catalog says "full sun." Finding the correct exposure involves putting the right plant in the right light. Since plant species vary in their need for light, match the plant's preference to your exposure for best results. There are plants that will grow well in all but the deepest shade. Even there, you can rotate containers of plants from other areas if you need color.

Easy access to water is vital, especially for growing plants from seed. Until they are well started, seedlings will need daily or twice-daily watering.

Gardens can be any size, but it is best to start small and then expand each year as you evolve a definite garden plan, gain experience, and improve your soil.

### MAKE SOIL IMPROVEMENT A HABIT

Organic matter such as peat moss or compost adds some nutrients and much water hold-ing capacity to Florida's sandy soil. Whether used as a mulch on top or dug into the soil, organic matter continually breaks down into humus and eventually disappears from the soil in any of the 50 states. It does so faster with Florida heat and rainfall. So make accumulation and replenishment of organic matter a constant part of your gardening. I figured years ago that mulching was easier and more effective than hoeing. And before long you can tell just by sticking a trowel into the soil how much it has improved from the humus and where more organic matter is needed.

### BUYING ORGANIC MATERIAL

If you are buying organic matter, probably the best kind for lasting usefulness is Canadian sphagnum peat moss. This comes in bales of various sizes. Before you use it, cut the bale open in a big "I" shape and pour in a bucket of warm water: five gallons for a four-cubic foot bale. Then close the plastic and let it sit overnight to moisten. And if it still seems too dry the next day, add more water from the hose. Peat retains from 12 to 30 times its weight in water retention, is sterile and weed free, and is easy to use. It provides an excellent environment for beneficial microbial growth in the soil.

However, it does not add any of the microbes or any nutrients, so use fertilizer now and begin gathering other organic matter and composting it as soon as possible, for future soil richness.

The old farmers were right: animal manure is great for the soil. When I found myself buying rabbit manure by the bagful, I decided to buy rabbits and produce it on the spot. Many horse stables offer free manure, but all my sons with trucks were still in Iowa and my spouse frowns on my hauling messy stuff in the car. At any garden center you can buy black cow manure by the bagful. This is all fine for starting your new garden, but is not necessary to keep buying organic matter while community waste departments are spending millions to haul away what we can use so well to improve our soil.

## BRINGING HOME THE LEAVES

"Please do not embarrass us by going around the neighborhood picking up grass clippings, Mom," my teenagers begged. I was a little embarrassed myself until I perfected my method. Now I wait until workers and school children leave on trash day and then set out. Within three blocks I can gather 30 bags of leaves or grass clippings or, best of all, mixtures of both, depending on the season. Some places put out bags of pure pine needles, a great looking mulch. Anything put out for trash collection is legal plunder and no one has questioned me in the five years I've been doing this. My embarrassment has largely disappeared and the trash men beg me to take more. One homeowner once helped me load his leaves and said, "There are several ladies who do this." And one fellow gardener stopped to say, "I wondered who else was smart enough to do what I do."

**Tips.** Do not leave these bags in the car for any length of time in Florida heat. I picked some up on the way to, instead of home from, a few hours' work to beat the trash trucks one day and it took months to get the smell out of the car.

Also, do not leave bags of hot grass clippings where they could start a fire. It isn't likely, but it has happened. Grass clippings were blamed for a barn fire that killed 30 race horses at the fairgrounds in my hometown in Ohio.

Do not put grass clippings in actual contact with plant parts or even close enough for a rain to wash them into contact. When combined with Florida heat, they can burn plants if they are still hot. Spread them out first and pull them well back from stems or leaves. After they dry enough to be cool, you can pull them closer.

Never use grass clippings from unknown sources around treasured plants. The clippings could contain herbicides, residues from someone else's lawn treatment. I have found the organic matter well worth the risk, but when in doubt I put clippings where I want to kill sod or on a spot that will not be planted for several weeks.

New laws against yard wastes in landfills are going to change things over the next few years. More people will be using chippers, shredders, and mulching mowers, then using the wastes as soil amendments and mulches. But as of today, many Florida homeowners are neater than they need to be. One neighbor gladly sends her sons for my garden cart whenever she cuts grass so she doesn't have to bag it and I don't have to unbag it. I felt compelled to tell her how the mulch would help her shrubbery. She said she knew that but preferred to buy woodchips by the truckload. This attitude should keep the rest of us well supplied.

## COMPOSTING

There are dozens of ways to make compost and you can't do it wrong, only more slowly. You can compost on the spot by letting organic mulch rot into the ground. It looks neater to cover a bucket of vegetable scraps from the kitchen with grass clippings or leaves.

Mix layers of dry and green material and add manure, compost activator, or something with nitrogen like cottonseed meal. These steps will heat the compost pile for better destruction of harmful bacteria and weed seeds and will hurry the process. Water and air are necessary, so when you are out with the hose, remember the compost pile. Turning speeds the decomposition, but this labor is not necessary. You can shovel finished compost from the bottom while you add new layers of organic matter to the top. The finished product takes a few weeks to a few months, depending on the season and the composition of the pile.

The smaller the bits of material, the quicker the decomposition of the pile, the less space it takes, and the neater it looks. I refuse to spend much time chopping garbage, but I know people who frappe theirs in the blender. It is easy to bring the lawn mower up and down over a pile of weeds or leaves and chop them into fine pieces. If you don't have a shredder, make a place behind a bush to pile branches and such. You can use some of them as stakes for supporting climbing or weak-stemmed plants.

## COVER CROPS

In any season, as soon as possible, start to work on the soil in your proposed planting beds. Even if you are not sure where the beds will go, you can't go wrong planting cover crops to improve the soil.

With cover crops you can grow large amounts of "green manure" on the spot in just a few weeks time. When you spade or till this into the soil, you add more pounds or tons of organic matter than you'd ever care to carry from the chicken coop.

Bill Saalman of the Soil Conservation Service says, "You will see plantings of sorghum and sesbania, a succulent legume, in the empty strawberry and vegetable fields in the summer."

The growers plow this down, then wait two to three weeks before replanting while the soil microbes work to turn the green manure into humus. You can till your cover crop in at any time, wait for two weeks, and then plant a garden of flowers, vegetables, or shrubs, or even a new lawn, that will be headed for easy success in the greatly improved soil.

anut

Different cover crops will do best in different seasons. If it is summer, plant black-eyed peas, crotalaria, hairy indigo, peanuts, sorghum, soybeans, or sudan grass. For fall planting, oats, amaranth, millet, soybeans, or rye grass are good. In early spring plant any kind of beans, more amaranth, buckwheat, millet, peanuts, or soybeans. Growing these will teach you much about Florida gardening and also about the micro-climates and soil variations in your yard.

Cover crops need water and nutrients, too. Even these soil-building plants won't grow very well in unimproved soil, but by growing them you will be taking a useful step forward and improving the soil in a new garden. If you decide later to move the bed and replant grass, the soil will be that much better.

For a dual purpose cover crop, use cowpeas or any kind of beans, including soybeans. Fertilize for a better crop. Sow a good edible variety and harvest whatever you can use. Then plow the rest into the soil.

If you don't have a tiller, you can mow off the cover crop, leave it as a mulch, put newspapers over the top and then add more mulch, as described below under *mulching instead of tilling.*

Summer is an ideal time to plant cover crops (and tropical pumpkins and cucuzzi) because other vegetables do not grow then and will not need the space. In the fall, when they do, their space will be much improved. Perennial covers or self sowers like amaranth, cowpeas, crotalaria, and indigo can be sown in groves or around fruit trees for long-term soil buildup. Mow these as often and as low as you wish for on-the-spot mulch production. Plant annual rye grass among spring corn and beans and it will loosen the soil, then die out as the days get hotter. Just leave the residue as mulch.

## TILLING

You can prepare your new planting ground by tilling to break up the sod. But before you begin, call the phone company and the cable TV company. They will gladly send someone out to locate underground cables and prefer to do so before you cut them.

It is best to till once and then let the area sit for a few days before tilling again. The days between tillings are an ideal time to spread as much as possible of sphagnum peat, grass clippings, leaves, sawdust, manure, or whatever soil improvers you can get over the ground. You can't get too much, though it is easier to till in a few inches at a time. If you don't have a tiller and don't wish to rent or hire one, there is another way.

You can remove sod from the area chosen for your garden without chemicals or hard labor. Just spread a heavy layer of grass clippings on it and keep it watered. In three weeks the grass sod below should be partly rotted and much easier to turn over. Dig in the clippings and sod, too.

## MULCHING INSTEAD OF TILLING

If you have neither tiller nor young muscles, you can carry the mulching method one step farther and never have to till the soil. Spread newspapers over the sod, where you want your garden. Overlap them so weeds can't creep in through the cracks. Over this, spread a thick layer of grass clippings and/or leaves. After watering well, you can then plant at once by pulling the mulch back to the newspapers and adding soil around the roots of individual plants

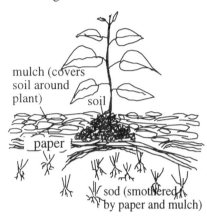

mulch (covers soil around plant)

soil

paper

sod (smothered by paper and mulch)

or over the top of seeds as needed. Holes for large plants can be dug through the newspapers, the bits of sod removed to the top layer of mulch, and the mulch pulled back up to the trunk after planting.

This method, perfected by ECHO (Educational Concerns for Hunger Organization, in Tampa) for use in third world countries, works very well for Florida gardeners. I have used it extensively for three years now. The roots will penetrate the newspapers when they need to. Meanwhile, the newspaper tends to keep the moisture and nutrients at root level and slow down their leaching through the sand. It also keeps the nematodes away from any roots formed in the mulch, blocks out weeds, and within a few months rots into the soil as humus, since paper came from trees originally.

The only problems with this method involve finding soil to add on top, the mulch sometimes smothering tiny plants, and eventual re-entry of some weeds, especially grasses. For soil you can use purchased potting soil or any combination of soil, compost, peat moss, perlite, or vermiculite that you would use in containers. This method takes less than is needed for container growing. Put cardboard or plastic milk cartons with bottoms cut away around young plants to mark them and protect them from shifting mulch. The weeds that enter are few compared to the number that sprout in unmulched soil.

**WATER RETAINING GELS**

I experimented with the addition to the soil of water retaining gels like Soil Moist (TM) and Terra Sorb (TM). The gel crystals absorb water and hold it in the root zone where it does the most good. The gels are especially effective in sandy, quick-drying soils.

Some products combine fertilizer with the gel, but what you gain in nutrients you lose in water holding capacity. In either form, these are slightly expensive. I ordered and used a pound of Soil Moist brand plus various samples.

The gel has such immense water-holding capacity that only a very minute amount can be dug in under a planting hole. If you add too much, it will expand and push the plant right up and out of the ground. The gel also can expand back to the surface of the soil, where it looks like cubes of Jello. If this happens, dig it in again right away. On the surface it quickly becomes useless. In the soil it is good for several months to over a year, and by that time permanent plants are well enough established not to need it so much.

dry crystals of water-retaining gel

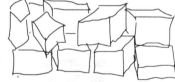

moistened crystals of water-retaining gel

In containers, especially in hanging pots, the addition of gel can make the difference between having to water twice a day or every two days. It also reduces stress on the plants and saves water. It is not a necessary additive, but it is something that you may find interesting to test in your own pots and garden.

**SOIL pH**

The soil pH is a measure of its alkalinity or acidity. A pH of 7.0 is neutral. Numbers below 7.0 indicate the degree of acidity; those above indicate its alkalinity. Most flowers and vegetables grow best in a slightly acid to neutral range. Trees and shrubs vary in their needs. Dogwoods, camellias, azaleas, hollies, and gardenias prefer acid soil.

Although virgin Florida soils can range from pH 3.8 (very acid) to pH 8.0 (quite alkaline), most Florida soils have a slightly acid to nearly neutral pH. If the soil is high in limestone or seashells, close to a new house, on manmade ground near the water, or in the Florida Keys, it may be quite alkaline.

Soil tests and advice are available from each county's agricultural extension office. So are the instructions for gathering samples. You can also buy a home testing kit, follow instructions, and do it yourself.

To tell the truth, I seldom test soil. Testing certainly makes for more exact feeding, higher yields, and fewer problems. It would definitely be a good idea to begin by having the soil in your new yard tested. But if your plants are growing well, the pH must be in a suitable range. If it is not, you will soon know by their declining attractiveness.

If the leaves of the gardenia turn pale, this is a sign that the roots need more acidity. Often watering with a product like Miracid (TM) will make a remarkable difference in just a few days. But such treatments will need to be continued indefinitely to maintain unnatural pH levels.

Pine needles, oak leaves, and peat moss make an alkaline soil more acid, but it takes huge amounts to make a difference. Large amounts of organic material will bring any soil close to neutral, correcting soil pH no matter which way it is wrong in the first place.

Chipped sulfur will make soil more acid much more easily. A temporary home remedy for overly alkaline soil is to add a tablespoon or two of vinegar to each gallon of water used for irrigation. Ground limestone makes soil more alkaline. It's rarely needed in Florida except for in the northernmost sections.

You can estimate a soil's pH by noticing which plants grow well in it. If your neighborhood or yard features flourishing azaleas, blueberries, strawberries, or other acid-lovers listed above, it indicates an acid soil. If these are conspicuous for their absence, alkaline soil may be the reason.

One very good plant to use for indicating soil pH is the common or "blue" hydrangea. Florist's hydrangeas sold as Easter plants are fine for this purpose. The flowers and bracts react to soil pH by changing colors. Oddly, the effect goes contrary to the coloration of litmus paper. Where the soil is acid enough for azaleas, the flowers will be blue. Where soil is neutral to alkaline, blooms will be pink. You can change the color of the bloom by adding aluminum sulfate to the soil to increase the acidity.

However, the hydrangeas I have planted have barely survived and are not yet grown enough to indicate anything. But there are several large and lovely ones in our area, all with blue or whitish blue blooms. Note that this plant generally needs plentiful supplies of water and fertilizer, and is often potbound when sold.

**TREATING FOR NEMATODES**

Nematodes are microscopic roundworms. Gardeners in northern states may hear about nematodes but never have to worry about them. In Florida, the harmful nematodes are a serious threat to many crops and ornamentals. When you pull out sickly looking beans and find swollen, knotted, gnarled roots, you are seeing a common kind of nematode damage. Nitrogen nodules on the roots of a healthy legume crop will easily rub off.

There are several ways to control nematodes. They are less prevalent in soil that is rich in humus, so adding plenty of organic matter may solve or at least stave off the problem. Very susceptible plants such as figs can be mulched knee high and do quite well. Mine have.

Nematodes are less likely to be a problem near a walk or the foundation of the house. In open ground they are most prevalent in the top 12 to 15 inches of the soil. One grower, Dr. Celso Gomez-Sanchez of Lutz, Florida, plants his figs in bottomless large pots that he fills with very rich organic soil and sinks into otherwise normal planting holes. The sides of the pot form a mechanical barrier that prevents most nematode damage and the open bottoms let the roots spread deeply into the soil.

Some plants are not bothered, and some varieties of susceptible plants are more resistant. Marigolds, impatiens, and native plants seem resistant, and sweet potatoes seem to repel nematodes. Most other plants are affected to some degree. The damage may be minimal your

first year, but increase in subsequent years.

There are two methods of eliminating most nematodes from an extensive planting area and both require a covering of clear plastic and waiting at least three weeks before planting. But one, fumigating with a chemical called Vapam, is no longer available to homeowners because it poses environmental hazards.

### SOLARIZATION

Many gardeners, including me, always did manage to get along without using such drastic measures. I never used Vapam, but I have used soil solarization as an alternative during the warm months. This involves preparing the soil as if for planting, raking it smooth, and watering it so that it is moist two feet deep. Then simply cover the area with 2- to 6-mil clear plastic and seal the edges well with soil, rocks, or such. A plastic paint dropcloth from Wal-Mart may not be quite as good, but it will do.

Gaps or air pockets will retard the heat buildup, though they are about impossible to eliminate completely. Allow four to six weeks for treatment, longer if a cool spell comes. Afterward allow the soil to dry to workable texture.

This "new" solarization method was developed in Israel and has been used extensively in California. Consider it if you have soil empty now or a new plot in mind to till.. In four to six weeks, soil can reach temperatures sufficient to kill many nematodes, weed seeds, and soil-borne fungi.

Solarizing the sod without tilling is safer around buried underground cables. Solarization works on small or large plots anywhere where the summer sun is hot enough, actually in most of the country. It is safe, inexpensive, nonchemical, leaves no plant-injuring residues, and is simple to apply. It kills many soil pests and brings favorable physical and chemical changes to the soil itself.

For better or worse, it does not kill everything. It can therefore be used around trees and shrubs without doing any damage to the tree roots. In tests, soluble nutrients such as calcium, nitrogen, magnesium, and potassium proved more available for plant use after treatment. Several beneficial soil microbes either survived the treatment or recolonized the area soon after. The net result was increased plant production that lasted for several years.

# CHAPTER FIVE
## GREEN GRASS AND OTHER GROUNDCOVERS

The first thing you will notice about lawns in Florida is that the grasses are different. They feel different underfoot. St. Augustine is very coarse and can make for difficult walking.

Florida lawns, with proper care, can be green and lovely for most of the year, the weeks or days just after frost the only exception. In my family, we qualify as poor lawnkeepers by Florida's exacting standards, but we still come much closer to having green, green grass here than we ever did in the North. Proper lawn care need not take a great deal of time. But it is more crucial in Florida to take the right steps when they are needed, or you could wind up with costly damage.

None of the Florida grasses will have as fine a texture, withstand as much neglect, or exhibit the comeback power that northern grasses do. Starve your turf here or let insects set in, and pretty soon you'll have patchy grass fading to none at all, with weeds coming in to fill the vacant patches. And since so many homeowners have professional lawn service, a sick stand of turf stands out in contrast.

Even successful grass growing can bring problems. St. Augustine grass builds up thatch that needs to be "verticut" every few years. You can let a professional do the job or rent a verticutter and do it yourself. The control of thatch will cut down on chinch bug infestations.

### CUT YOUR LAWN DOWN TO SIZE

There are good reasons for decreasing the size of you lawn. Turf takes more water, mowing, and care than any other type of planting. Also, there are only a few varieties of grasses that will tolerate light to moderate shade. None will grow in heavy shade. That is all right, because we treasure the shade for certain flowers, ferns, ground covers, and shrubs that thrive there with a minimum of care. Many lovely ground covers (some of which are well known as houseplants) grow rapidly. And where you don't want to grow anything, mulches of leaves, pine needles, or tanbark can be quite attractive.

It is possible to have a small and attractive yard here with no grass at all. I've seen some with white rock mulch, ground covers, and shrubs surrounding a pool whose owners got rid of their lawnmower.

Most of us want some green lawn. But half an acre can be ridiculous. So while the neighbors are working to manicure their lawns, I am busy reducing mine to a workable size.

### WARM SEASON GRASSES

Unlike northern grasses that can be combined for various purposes, only one kind of warm-season grass will grow on any given area (winter exception to be explained later). You must select just one, or at the most one for each section of your yard. We inherited St. Augustine grass in the front yard and bahia (pronounced ba-HAY-ah) in the back. About 80 percent of Florida lawns are comprised of one or the other of these two grasses. If you live on the coast, you'll probably have St. Augustine, for it is the most salt tolerant. If you have no automatic irrigation, you will want bahia, for it withstands drought the best.

**BAHIA** (*Paspalum notatum*) is probably the least expensive and least troublesome. It can also be the least attractive. It is a coarse, pasture type of grass with an open habit that lets in weeds. It tolerates almost anything: sun or partial shade, neglect, heavy traffic, dry or moist, humid conditions, and acid or alkaline soil. It also resists pests and diseases. It turns brown below 30 degrees . In spring and summer it grows so quickly that it is hard to control the seedheads. A friend who moved into her Florida house in July saw the lawn in full seed and thought it had been neglected for weeks, but it was only bahia grass in bloom a week after the last mowing.

You can start bahia grass from seed. It is good enough for our backyard for now, but sometimes I'm glad no one can see inside the fence. Our neighbors have it in their front yard and care for it very well. Although it does not look as lush as some of the more pampered St. Augustine lawns on the block, it never looks as bad as the neglected ones.

Argentine, Paraguay, and Pensacola are improved varities, with Argentine the most popular because it has fewer seedheads. After preparing the ground well, sow 5 to 10 pounds of scarified seed to every 1000 square feet.

**BERMUDA GRASS** (*Cynodon dactylon*) is a lovely, dark green, fine in texture, and like a cloud to walk on, the closest to northern grasses we have here. This is what they use on the golf courses, with special varieties for the greens. There is a nearby apartment complex where it is well kept and quite attractive. But, for most homeowners, it takes too much care: mowing twice a week in summer, feeding eight times a year, and weeding and watering all the time. It is more resistant to pests than St. Augustine, but still needs spraying at the first sign of dollar spot fungus, and autumn treatment for army worms (sod webworms). It will not grow in shade. Start it with plugs, sprigs, or sod.

### CENTIPEDE GRASS

(*Eremochloa ophiuroides*) has a medium green color and texture and takes less mowing (every ten days in summer) and feeding than the others. It works well on the heavier soils of northern Florida but suffers from nematodes in the rest of the state. It is not tolerant of drought, salt, or heavy traffic, and turns brown in winter. Start this from sprigs, plugs, or seed, and watch out for ground pearls, cousins of the mealy bug.

Cut apart rooted sections of stolons (sprigs), and replant where needed.

**ST. AUGUSTINE** (*Stenotaphrum secundatum*) is a coarse-textured grass with an attractive deep blue-green color year round except for a few days after any freeze. It has few seedheads and is the most shade, salt, and cold tolerant. It needs ample moisture and feeding, especially under trees. It tends to build up spongy thatch that makes walking difficult and will deteriorate quickly if insects and diseases are not constantly controlled. Chinch bugs are its number one enemy and can wipe out large areas if untreated. Mow most forms of this grass only to three inches, 'Seville' to two inches. 'Floratum,' 'Bitterblue,' and 'FX-10' are improved varieties.

**ZOYSIA** (*Zoisia* species) is tolerant of salt air and has a dense, lush, hardy growth. However, it is much slower growing than the others and may take up to two years to fill in completely after plugging. It is therefore also less invasive to surrounding plantings. Though durable under traffic, it is not resistant to nematodes and takes careful soil preparation, plentiful watering and feeding, and frequent mowing to thrive. The new variety 'Cashmere' is more tolerant of shade and faster growing, and quite lovely.

## FLORIDA LAWN GRASSES AT A GLANCE

| Grass type, care needed | Texture | Winter color | Shade tolerance | Problems |
|---|---|---|---|---|
| **St. Augustine.** Start from plugs or sod. | Very coarse | Green* | Filtered shade | Many |
| **Bahia.** Start from seed. | Medium | Green | Very light shade | Few |
| **Bermuda.** Needs most care. | Finest | Green* | None | Many |
| **Centipede.** Nematode problems may limit use. | Medium | Brown | Moderate shade | Few |
| **Zoysia.** Slow to spread | Medium fine | Green* | Moderate shade | Few |

*Can be green most of the year with proper care.

CARPET GRASS (*Axonopus affinis*) will survive in moist soil under pine trees, where it requires only spring feeding and two or three mowings a summer. It turns brown in winter, likes acid soil, produces branching flower stalks, and can be started from seed, sod, or plugs.

WINTER GRASSES, sown right over any of the perennial types mentioned, will give you a beautiful green lawn like you dreamed of up north all winter long. Sow in October or November. Annual rye grass will last until May and then die out automatically. Such lawns stand out for their color and prevent weeds from getting started in the permanent grass, but they also mean mowing all winter as well as all summer. They can require irrigation during dry spells and ought to be fed in December or January. If you decide you want a green lawn that much, sow five to ten pounds of Italian rye grass seed per 1,000 square feet. Rye is the usual choice, but you can also sow two pounds of Kentucky bluegrass, or use one pound of bent grasses for shady areas.

## CALENDAR:
## LAWN CHORES FOR FLORIDA

**January-February.** Mow, weed, and water as needed. Mowing can be as infrequent as every two or three weeks during these months.

**March-April.** Feed with a high-nitrogen fertilizer like 16-4-8, cottonseed meal, manure tea, or Lawn Restore (TM). Apply according to label directions or spread about six pounds of the first two every 1,000 square feet. Treat weeds. You may want to feed a second time four to six weeks later. Be careful not to overfeed as this causes a rush of tender new grass that insects can hardly resist. Begin watching for insect damage, especially from mole crickets, chinch bugs, and sod webworms. At the first sign of any pest or disease, water with one cup liquid soap in a 20-gallon hose-end sprayer. Then get detailed material from your extension office and treat pests accordingly.

**May.** Use diatomaceous earth to help control both chinch bugs and lawn fleas. Scanmask (TM) treats chinch bugs and nematodes. This month can still be very hot and dry. If so, it is a crucial time for watering. Begin planning to make the best use of the summer rainy season by getting lawn repair work started.

**June-September.** These are the rainy months and grass will need mowing once a week, every week. St. Augustine can be kept at three to four inches. Try to never cut off more than one third of the top growth, for this will result in yellowing and sun scald. The new mulching mowers cut grass clippings and leaves into small pieces for faster decomposition, but clippings from any mower can be left and will enrich the lawn as long as you don't let the grass get too tall before mowing. For extra greening without extra growth, you can apply iron sulfate according to label instructions once or twice at four to six week intervals, starting in July. Check lawn mower blades for sharpness at least once a month. Continue to watch for diseases and insects and to water if needed. Natural rainfall will usually be enough.

**August or September.** Feed again.

**October to December.** Mow, water, and treat insect or disease problems as needed. Enjoy respite when not.

**Any Time.** Remove thatch by raking, renting a power rake for bahia, a verticutter for St. Augustine, or hiring a professional. This is a must at least every few years with St. Augustine grass. Afterwards, rake up the debris for the compost pile. Open and dampen a bag of sphagnum peat (see page 23) in the middle of your lawn or section of lawn. Mix with bagged cow manure or compost in little piles all over the area, then rake in to improve the soil and increase water-holding capacity.

## PLUGGING FOR REPAIR OR A NEW LAWN

Any newcomer with an established lawn would do well to take care of whatever is there at first. Study the lawns you admire in the area and the different grasses displayed as plugs at nurseries. If you eventually want to change grass types or improve or repair what you have, plugging is the least expensive and easiest way for all the runner grasses: St. Augustine, zoysia, and Bermuda.

After dethatching and just before the summer rainy season is an excellent time to put in grass plugs, but it can be done all year round. Plugs are sold in trays holding 18. Order ahead if you want a large quantity at once. Each tray will cover 30 to 50 square feet. Another of the advantages of plugging is that you can do a small area at a time rather than a whole section or lawn.

While you are at the nursery, buy plug starter, a specially formulated fertilizer to put in the bottom of the holes. And rent or borrow a plugging tool. For a small job a hand plugger works nicely and lets you dig standing upright. If you are doing a large yard all at once, you can get an auger-like attachment for an electric drill.

Grass plugs are sold by the tray.

You can plug a runner-spreading grass like St. Augustine, for instance, among a seed-spreading grass like bahia, weeds and all. Leave the original grass growing but mow it low, about 1 1/2 inches.

You can even replace one runner-spreading grass with another, like St. Augustine with zoysia. In this case you must first kill the old lawn with a foliar weed killer like RoundUp(TM) or KleenUp (TM). Follow the instructions and wait the allotted time before replanting, usually two weeks. This will take the life out of grass and weeds without poisoning the soil. Then plug your new lawn right into the debris of the old one, which will decompose as the new grass runners cover it.

**PREPARE THE SOIL WELL**

For a new lawn, prepare the soil, tilling it deeply and working in peat moss, compost, and lime if needed, as you would for seeding. Add fertilizer. If using 6-6-6, apply ten pounds per 1,000 square feet. You may also want to treat for nematodes (see chapter 4).

At first the plugs will be lined up like a crop in rows. But before you know it, the empty spaces become green. Some of this will be weed growth, but don't worry. Grasses that come in plugs spread by runners and will take over with a thickness that seeded grasses seldom achieve. Depending on the kind, the season, and the care,

thick coverage takes three months for most types, up to two summers for zoysia.

Joe Kellerson, a retired man from New York now living in Riverview, Florida, made his St. Augustine lawn the showplace of the neighborhood, redoing it himself a little at a time. He usually bought and worked with ten plug trays each trip.

"Pick out the greenest, healthiest looking trays," he says. You can stack them up in the back of your car without any mess. One day I put in 17 trays."

The day before you work on a section of lawn, water the area well so that it is damp down a good three or four inches: about 45 minutes with most automatic sprinkler systems, up to a few hours with hose-end systems. This will soften the soil and cut your digging time and effort by as much as half and also get the plugs off to the best possible start. Watering a day in advance leaves the soil moist, but means that it is well enough drained that you do not have to work in wetness.

Kellerson recommends watering the plugs in their trays well, too. Then turn them upside down. The plugs are tough; you don't have to be gentle. Sometimes the runners have already spread enough to root into other sections. Use force to pull them apart or cut connections. If some roots on the runners are exposed, you can either cover them or not. The main root ball will sustain growth until the runners take root again.

Kellerson set his plugs about 18 inches apart in a checkerboard pattern.

"Where the ground was almost bare, I measured exactly. But where there was some lawn already, I filled in the empty spots as close to that as possible."

Zoysia grass grows more slowly, so plug it every ten to twelve inches. The closer you plant, the quicker the covering.

You can remove the soil from the holes to other areas of the yard or to the compost pile. Or break it up and spread it between the holes after they are planted. The drill attachment pulverizes the soil from the hole so it is easy to spread.

Be careful about hitting tree roots with the auger. Also be sure to count plugs and fill up every hole. If you accidentally leave one empty, someone could turn an ankle.

Keep the plugs moist at all times until rooted. The first three weeks are critical. Do not sprinkle as for grass seed, but water deeply for roots that are three inches deep.

Plugs settle in as quickly as in seven to ten days. Tug on the top of a plug. If it does not come up, it is time to shift from daily to every-other-day watering.

When plugs have begun to take root, mowing becomes very important to encourage branching and runners instead of height. Apply lawn food every four to six weeks after installation for three applications. Continue to water and mow as needed.

## LAWNMOWER CARE

Lawnmower care is the same as in the North, but you don't change for winter. Oil needs changing and mower blades need sharpening more often in Florida.

## LAWN CARE COMPANIES

There are many lawn care professionals in Florida, and you may wish to employ them, especially in your first year until you become familiar with the new grasses and the problems you might expect. If you want as few poison chemicals anywhere on your property as possible, it will be more difficult to find the right company. Shop around until you find a lawn care service that will use organic products and explain why, as they do it.

## LAWN ALTERNATIVES

In Florida, lawns need a lot more than just mowing, because the soils lack fertility and water holding capacity, and there is a wide array of pests and diseases. So, consider alternatives to a large lawn. Marianne Binetti, in her book, *Tips for Carefree Landscapes*, suggests that you stick your sprinkler into the middle of your lawn, turn it on high, and then keep whatever gets wet for your lawn. Around the edges, set in drought-resistant ground covers or mulch with something attractive like tan wood chips, small bark chips, pine needles, white gravel, or black chunks of coal. Binetti lives in the Pacific Northwest where it is almost always rainy. Her advice is that much more practical for our rainy desert in Florida.

I have seen several yards where large areas of wood bark mulch are part of the design, but also serve as extra parking spaces or a turn-around area. This is an excellent idea, attractive and, on busy streets where backing out is a problem, a significant safety feature. It combines low-maintenance landscaping with better access into or out of long streams of traffic.

## GROUND COVERS INSTEAD

Ground covers make lovely lawn substitutes that add color, texture, elegance, and ease. In Florida most are evergreen. They can be flowering, fragrant, drought-resistant, pest-free, and perfectly delightful. Some of them will take a bit of foot traffic. In the others you can put stepping stones or paths of pine needles.

While paving and light colored mulches reflect heat and can add to air conditioning costs, lawns and ground covers absorb heat and shade the ground.

Ground covers take a bit of watering until established and through their first dry season. New plantings will need roughly the same weeding as a flower or vegetable garden through their first summer. This will diminish to only a bit of hand weeding as they spread and crowd out the competition. They will grow and prosper where grass will not.

Look over the following list of ground covers quickly. Then, on your first trip to a nursery, buy one or two pots of whichever ones you like, as a test. Plant them in your first enriched ground, in sun or shade as needed, and let them start spreading. By the time you have your landscape plan settled, you'll know what will grow best and spread fastest for you and will have a good start on your planting stock. Divide or take cuttings of the original plants and plant a small area at a time for the least expense. Or buy what you need and plant it all at once. Or watch for a gardener thinning an overcrowded groundcover planting, and ask for starter plants that would otherwise be thrown away.

## GROUNDCOVERS FOR FLORIDA

**Asparagus fern** (*Asparagus sprengeri*) grows so readily in all areas of Florida, in full sun or partial shade, that some people consider it a weed. It gets 12 to 24 inches tall and each plant can spread to four feet in width. It is cold-hardy in zone 9, fairly salt-tolerant, and very drought tolerant. The fernlike foliage is a bright green and it has tiny pink or white flowers followed by red berries. Chances are the birds will drop a few seeds and you'll find some starts whether you want them or not. Otherwise any neighbor who has some will be glad to share.

**Blue daze** (*Evolvulus nuttallianus*) is a Florida treasure that I bought right away for its lovely blue flower. Strangely, few of the other Florida gardening books mention it, except Lewis Maxwell who says it has good salt tolerance but is cold tender. I know it grows easily in sun or shade, stays about ten inches tall, spreads quickly, and is moderately drought tolerant. It has blue flowers that open only part of the day, but open every day that is above freezing. A fertilizer low in N, high in P and K will increase bloom. The foliage is small, oval, and gray-green. My first pot spread over large areas before it died out in a freeze. The second one lasted three years and spread even further.

**Bugleweed** (*Ajuga reptans*) is as hardy all over Florida, in full sun or partial shade, as it is in the North, and it spreads faster. Except while in bloom, it grows only a few inches tall, but a single plant multiplies into many and will soon spread one to three feet. The upright blue spires of flowers show up from February through April, and there are  several available varieties with different foliage colors. The most common is a deep green that turns bronze in the winter. Ajuga has poor salt tolerance.

**Ferns** of many kinds do well as ground covers in shade to partial sun, throughout the state. The ones we tried and killed back in our dry, heated, northern houses will carpet the

ground beneath trees and even climb the trunks of some of the palms here. Don't let them take over a flower garden, but give them beds of their own, where they will do well as ground covers. They are ideal under oaks with only occasional watering.

**Honeysuckle**, Halls and trumpet (*Lonicera japonica* and *L. sempervirens*), will grow in northern and central Florida as vines or ground covers. Only the first, with white flowers turning yellow, is fragrant. The pink flowers of the other have little odor. Florida soil and humidity tame these in our area. They are hardy and consistently poking through my neighbor's fence. But the cuttings I've taken have grown very slowly, much to my astonishment. In Pennsylvania we were careful not to park where this could cover our car while we were gone.

**Hottentot Fig** (*Carpobrotus edulis*) is a creeping succulent that is a moderately drought tolerant, shore or open sun ground cover for central and southern Florida. Its gray-green, creeping leaves grow six inches tall. Yellow or rose-purple daisylike flowers bloom in summer.

**Ivies** (*Hedera helix* and *H. canariensis*) are excellent ground covers for all of Florida. They thrive even in the deep shade of oak trees, and will climb trunks without damaging them. Ivy has moderate salt tolerance. One lady put a sad looking 15 cent plant beside a tree and it grew to cover a large section of the yard and curtain the tree most attractively with enough extra to supply a local florist occasionally. There are hundreds of varieties of ivy with different leaf shapes, colors, sizes, and markings. Ivy requires water, and sometimes there are problems with scale or spider mites.

**Jasmine**. Several jasmines, though most often grown as shrubs or vines, may be allowed to sprawl as ground covers.
Star jasmine (*Jasminum nitidum*) is hardy to 30 degrees F and will come back after a cold spell. It needs sun and will grow fairly fast. The delicate, starlike flowers open from pink

buds and are fragrant, especially morning and night. They continue blooming intermittently from spring to frost. These have poor salt tolerance and need some pruning to keep neat and shapely.

Confederate jasmine (*Trachelospermum jasminoides*) is hardy in all of Florida, likes sun for best bloom, but will tolerate deep shade. It grows slowly to climb or spread 20 feet and is covered with very fragrant white, twisty-shaped 3/4 inch flowers from February to May. There is also a variety with variegated leaves. This one is quite salt tolerant.

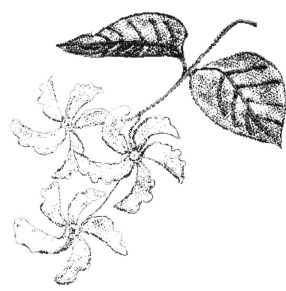

**Joseph's coat** (*Alternanthera amoena*) is hardy if protected from frost in central and southern Florida. In full sun or partial shade, plants grow five to ten inches tall and spread quickly 12 to 24 inches. The leaves are multicolored with pink, red, green, and cream. Flower spikes appear in spring, but are not showy. Occasional problems with caterpillars can be treated with *Bt*. Plants are not salt-tolerant.

**Junipers** (*Juniperus* species) are hardy all over Florida and are the best of the needled, coniferous (cone-bearing) evergreen ground-covers. They do best in full sun to partial shade. Some are shrubs or trees, but many are sprawling to prostrate ground covers growing from slowly to moderately fast, staying as low as six inches tall, and spreading from three to eight feet. One of the best ground covers is the shore juniper with blue-green foliage and good salt tolerance.

Some cultivars have foliage with decorative yellow tips. Junipers sometimes have problems with spider mites or juniper blight, but are drought tolerant. They seldom fruit in Florida.

**Kalanchoe** (*Kalenchoe* species) can be used as an interesting succulent ground cover for southern Florida, and in protected spots in the central area. Drought tolerant, It needs full sun to light shade. Some types have lovely blooms for several weeks from Christmas to spring. These are fairly salt tolerant. Take cuttings if it frosts. They will root lying on top of wet sand.

**Lantana**. Creeping lantana (*Lantana montevidensis*) grows wild and slightly woody where protected from frost in much of Florida. In the north it dies to the ground but comes back quickly in the spring. It blooms best in full sun but does well in shade also, especially under orange trees. The flowers, in colors of orange, yellow, lavender, pink, and cream, are abundant in the summer but also for much of the rest of the year. Plants have excellent salt and drought tolerance and the leaves and stems have a delightful fragrance when crushed or brushed.

**Lilyturf** (*Liriope muscari*) is hardy in all sections of the state and all soils in the shade. Its grassy leaves grow 12 to 18 inches tall and crowns spread slowly to 30 inches. It blooms with lavender spikes of flowers in spring and summer, followed by black berries, showier than mondo grass. There are improved forms and some have variegated leaves. Creeping lilyturf (*Liriope spicata*) has purple to white flowers and spreads faster than muscari. All are moderately salt tolerant and very drought tolerant.

**Mondo grass** (*Ophiopogon japonicus*) looks much the same as liriope, though leaves may be shorter, more slender, and darker green. It is sometimes called dwarf lilyturf and I still

confuse the two lookalikes. So do some nurseries. Mondo grass is hardy and adaptive, growing in sun to full shade. It has lilac flowers in summer, though they are often hidden in the foliage. It has high salt tolerance. Both mondo grass and lilyturf are fine ground covers in the shade, often used for edging.

**Oyster plant** (*Tradescantia spathacea*, also known as *Rhoeo spathacea*) looks something like a stiffer form of purple wandering jew. It is the same genus as the one we called Moses-in-a-boat as a houseplant up north. It is hardy in central and southern Florida in sun or shade. It will freeze down but usually comes back, and it is drought tolerant. The deep green and purple foliage is lovely under pink crape myrtles. Its own flowers are inconspicuous.

**Periwinkle.** Madagascar periwinkle, often referred to as vinca, is now officially *Catharanthus roseus*. This drought and salt-tolerant plant is hardy in the central and southern sections of

the state, in sun or shade. It is grown as an annual in northern Florida, and in states farther north. Plants from cuttings or seeds spread quickly and grow up to two feet tall and wide. It blooms prolifically all summer and much of the rest of the year with white, pink, or lilac flowers on shiny, dark green foliage. Some varieties stay

shorter. Pinch back when small for bushiness. *Vinca minor* grows well in northern Florida.

**Society garlic** (*Tulbaghia violacea*) is similar to liriope and mondo grass, but with lilac flowers in sprays atop long stems rather than on spikes. It tolerates either sun or shade, but salt only slightly. The whole plant is edible and may be used like chives. It is not as commonly used, but leaves have a garlic fragrance and flavor when crushed.

**Wandering Jew** (*Zebrina pendula*) grows only four to ten inches tall. It is hardy in the central and southern areas, and requires shade and moist soil. Leaves have various stripes of purple, green, or white.

Many other plants do well as ground covers here, including daylilies, dichondra, coontie, and creeping figs, in all parts of the state. Aloe, bromeliads, beach morning glory, and wedelia grow in central and southern zones. So do northern houseplants like Chinese evergreen, pothos, and philodendron. Creeping charlie and partridgeberry, and winter creeper grow in northern zones. Artillery plant grows well in southern Florida.

# CHAPTER SIX
# FLOWERS IN FLORIDA

Florida gets its name from its abundance of flowers. Hundreds of species, both natives and new arrivals, thrive here and richly color the seasons. Some will be familiar to you, some new.

You can still grow most of your old favorites, but plant them at different times of year than you did in the North. Some flowers, especially hardy perennials, will not do well here because of the weather, and you'll be glad to know in advance that it is not your fault! Others will thrive without too much care. Right away, you will start learning the names and needs of the intriguing new flower you see around you.

## HANDS-ON EXPERIENCE

Seedlings of old favorites like salvia and nasturtium sat in my first flowerbeds that whole first summer and sulked. Looking back, I wonder that they survived. I had no idea then that, come winter, those same seedlings would take off, grow, and bloom abundantly. As with vegetables, timing is all important (use the chart of planting times on page 41 as a guide).

On the other hand, the moonflowers that I had tried for years to grow in Iowa, with the most limited success, now grew and lit up the night. These cousins of the morning glory have larger blooms of a delicate white, open in the evening, and fill the air with their heavenly perfume. They are natives of Florida swamps, and the best way to raise them is to move to Florida. Many other exotic "wishbook" flowers are equally suited to growing conditions here.

Right from the beginning, I was learning from my mistakes. Nothing makes more of an impression or helps a person learn more quickly than hands-on experience. Luckily, with flowers, experience is not expensive. Of course, seed is cheap. You can also start with bedding plants and have an instant garden. And you are sure to have some successes right from the start. I've never had such globe amaranths as I grew that first summer.

## ASK OTHER GARDENERS

One of the houses we looked at was set in a paradise of trees, shrubs, and blooming flowers. It was not far from our new house. When I called and asked if I could have a garden tour, the owner, Mrs. Georgia, agreed readily. Most gardeners are flattered by such requests. I am.

Among the things I learned from her were that impatiens will continue to bloom from year to year in central Florida unless there is a severe freeze. In that case, plants come back readily from seed where the ground is kept moist enough. Or you can easily start them from seed or cuttings. The same is true of coleus. And she told me that caladiums need not be dug up in the winters except in the coldest parts of northern Florida. In central and southern regions, they die down in winter and come back reliably in spring.

Here is a hint I pass along, in the same spirit as the advice: "too much money can be a problem." Often the plants that people are glad to share are invasive growers, so be careful about accepting garden gifts and don't let anything overrun your space. Mrs. Georgia gave me a start of false roselle that has dark red leaves and darker red hibiscus-like flowers. All parts are edible and useful for making drinks or mixing in salads. I like it, but the plant goes crazy. Fortunately it dies back in the slightest freeze, but a million seedlings come up to replace it. Now I've learned to hoe out seedlings and prune branches mercilessly to keep it in its place, and warn anyone to whom I give starts.

Mrs. Georgia also gave me names of and directions to her favorite nurseries. Look for the same information from an experienced gardener who lives near your Florida home.

## NURSERIES AND GARDEN CENTERS

Before we moved, I bought a few plants every spring and a few supplies throughout the year. The people at the local garden center knew me because I asked so many questions and wrote columns about the answers. Since coming to Florida, the people at the nurseries are less likely to know me but likely to make more profit from my visits. I figured that I had left many plants behind, and anything I buy here is an investment in learning as well as landscaping. I am now too old to be frugal and learn slowly.

I find nurseries a great place to learn. Most feature plants labeled with the botanical and common name, whether to plant in sun or shade, and how tall the plant will grow. Don't hesitate to walk around with a notebook writing all this down so you can remember it.

Most reliable nurseries will sell the bedding plants appropriate for the coming season. If everything in my yard freezes, I go shopping the next day and at least get plants to add color by the front walk.

## READ ALL YOU CAN

I mentioned the county agricultural extension service in chapter 1, and recommend visiting the extension office often. Local newspapers are also good sources of timely information, but be careful to look for the work of Florida writers. Some papers take articles off the wire services that are not oriented to Florida. Some tips are relevant and some are ridiculous, but a newcomer does not know the difference at first.

Before I had been here many weeks, I got a surprise present in the mail from someone I had never met. Betty Mackey, who heard from a magazine editor with whom we both worked that I had moved, sent me a copy of her book, *A Cutting Garden for Florida.* It was small and specific, and helped me in growing cut flowers, and everything else, too. Betty moved North from Longwood, Florida just after I moved South, so when she wanted to expand the book a few years later, she asked me to be her coauthor. My garden bloomed with new and old favorite flowers while I researched that book, and continues to bloom because of it.

For anyone interested primarily in growing flowers, reading that book is the logical next step after this one. And the other books listed in chapter 1 would be next.

## LEARN AS YOU GROW

That first summer I had only the slightest inkling of all the factors of Florida growing mentioned in the third chapter. If you read or reread them now, they will save you many problems. But one of the most important parts of adjusting is to make some mistakes and learn from them. Don't let them discourage you. You will overcome most of that unsettled, unrooted feeling by the end of the first year (but you can still use it as an excuse for years). Relax and enjoy your garden. Here are some suggestions for flowers to grow in all seasons, and tips to make them bloom abundantly.

## Autumn

Experienced Florida gardeners think of fall as the start of the garden season, but you can stretch this notion from August to October. Before September, when the rains stop, it is still very easy to root cuttings, so propagate any of those bedding plants you bought. When the rains stop, remember to sprinkle or mist the cuttings every day. Prepare your soil while you are waiting for the season to change. One morning you will wake up and go out to feel wonderful coolness again. Then you can turn off the air conditioning, open the doors and windows, and intensify your gardening. Seedlings thrive in the cooler weather, in autumn sunlight that is not too intense for them. Mature plants spring out of the doldrums into new leaf and bloom.

In southern Florida, you can continue to grow summer annuals all fall and winter. Here in central Florida, I still take a chance on any I want. The weather varies considerably from year to year, and during the last two winters we have lost very little to cold. In northern and central Florida, you can enjoy chrysanthemums, which can be transplanted at any time of year. Most bloom both in fall and in spring.

You'll see petunias, dianthus, and pansies for sale in the fall, and these will bloom through most or all of the winter. Pansies are the most impervious to frost. The other two will lose flowers, but not leaves, to light frost unless protected from it.

In the northwestern counties, only the pansies have a chance of blooming all through the winter; the others will freeze very late in fall. As if in exchange, gardeners here have a climate cool enough for bearded iris, peonies, and other hardy perennial flowers we loved farther north but cannot grow in central and southern Florida.

In all parts of Florida, fall is a good time to sow seeds of biennials, perennials, and hardy annuals. In northern Florida, plant in September. Possibilities are violas, *Phlox drummondii*, alyssum, poppies, stocks, corn-flowers, rudbeckia, larkspur, baby's breath, snapdragon, and sweet peas. In central and southern Florida, sow seeds after the weather turns milder, in October or even November. Plant those flowers listed above plus nasturtiums, silene, jewels of Opar, sunflowers, clarkia, and California poppies.

The seeds grow slowly. A few will bloom in fall and winter, others not much until February or March, but then they start growing rapidly and will be large and vigorous plants that will give you flowers by the bunch.

### Winter

In a good year, we hardly notice that winter has come in central and southern Florida, except for the changes in day length and sun and shade patterns. Fall tends to melt into spring. Northern Florida has a more definite winter, but it is a fairly mild one, especially in contrast to states farther north.

Some of the trees, the sycamore, liquid-ambar (sweet gum), nothern fruits, and shrubs like crape myrtle, will lose their leaves and let in more sunlight. January is the closest we come to the dormancy of a northern winter, so if you have to move any woody or perennial plants, do it then. In southern Florida, it is the best time of year to plant bulbs, tubers and corms of flowers such as gladiolus, caladium, dahlia, amaryllis, crinum, and rain lily. Wait a few weeks longer in central Florida. In northern Florida, wait until danger of frost passes.

In all regions, prune flowering shrubs before new growth starts. Until you have lived here long enough to know when that is for sure, prune when you are in the mood or when you see swelling buds or new growth just starting. Or do it when you see your neighbors, the ones whose yards you admire, do theirs.

In northern Florida, bring in the plants you want to save from frost. They will need protec-tion for a few weeks, at least, usually from mid-December to February or March. Start your seedlings on the windowsill, in a sunroom, in a coldframe, or under lights indoors.

In much of the state, you can sow seeds all winter and only bring in plants if it gets cold enough to threaten frost. On the other hand, many plants that lived through winter in the North may die out here in a sudden frost, simply because it is so sudden, and the plant has not pre-pared for cold by sending sap safely to the roots.

### Spring

The main difference between spring here and spring farther north is that Florida's spring is the glorious end for many plants, rather than the beginning. So it is even more important to make the most of it. Starting plants in the fall and winter helps here. Then they are all ready to bloom with the first warmth. In South Florida, that can come in January as days start to length-en. Almost any annual flower will bloom and grow in Florida's spring, and a few of them are heat lovers that will continue into or through summer.

You will soon see that many plants actually bloom themselves to death here, without winter weather to finish them off. Some, like pentas, impatiens, coleus, vincas, and butterflyweed,

---

### Favorite plants that were new to me in Florida:

**Abelmoschus.** This needs a better name, but that is its only fault. *Abelmoschus moschatus* hybrids, hibiscus relatives, were new from Park Seeds about the time we moved, so I they may thrive in the North now as well. Seedlings started my first year have been blooming here ever since. They die back in a frost but always come back either from seeds or from the tuberous roots of older plants. They get about 19 inches tall and have only a few blooms at a time in lovely shades of coral pink or cherry red. The leaves are dark green, reddish in the winter, and deeply, palmately lobed. Flowers are about two inches across and only last a day, but they are very striking. So are the dried seedpods. Plant in full sun in early spring in northern Florida, anytime in central and southern Florida. This makes a lovely low hedge.

**Bishop's Flower.** This is one to plant for white clouds of bloom in spring. I ordered Queen Anne's lace, but J. L. Hudson (seed company) sent me this, *Ammi majus*, instead. I was disappointed until it started to bloom. Wow! Seeds planted in fall grow slowly until spring, then take off. The plants have shiny, compound leaves which are less coarse, feathery, or carrot-scented than Queen Anne's lace. The flowers are similar, but there is no dark floret in the center, and there are many more flower clusters per plant for quite a show from early April until late May. Some of the plants grew six feet tall and needed staking. It is best to pinch them back at least once. Ammi is excellent for cutting, and now the pros are raising it for florist flowers. Sometimes it is said to be perennial, but mine are biennial. The plants bloom themselves to death and do not reseed, so I start a new batch every fall.

### Salvias I Never Saw Before

The demonstration garden at the Extension Office yielded my first cutting of Mexican sage, *Salvia leucantha*, and it has grown in my garden ever since. It has many white stems with long, narrow, textured, gray-green leaves that can grow as tall as four feet. Each stem starts opening a showy spire of white flowers surrounded by vivid lavender calyces. These last indefinitely and can be hung to dry. Cut stems back after flowering and a new bunch will come up from the crown. These root easily from softwood cuttings. Give Mexican sage full sun, enriched soil, and room to spread. It looks good with pentas. Plants are fairly carefree, but need water and flower fertilizer occasionally.

Several other sages that thrive in Florida gardens include:

*Salvia farinacea*, blue or mealy-cup sage. Though it is grown as an annual in the North, it is a perennial here. Plants can be removed and replaced after their first flush of blooms if you wish. 'Indigo Spires' is a hybrid with dark blue blooms.

*Salvia uliginosa*, or bog salvia, grows in a large clump and 4 to 5 feet tall with lovely, ice-blue spires in early summer.

*Salvia elegans*, pineapple sage, has deep red, edible flowers and fragrant foliage. Thompson & Morgan offers 'Starry Eyed' mix, including types with white, salmon, and scarlet blooms. A slightly leggier form, *Salvia coccinea,* grows wild in my yard and throughout Florida. It is more orange red than the blue-red of pineapple sage, does not have much scent, and blooms from frost to frost with little care, only occasional pruning. I now also have other salvias, one with yellow spires, and two different forms of dark blue. I have seen lovely pinks, too. I recommend trying any salvia in your Florida garden.

just keep on blooming and always look good. Picking bunches for the house encourages more growth. Prune plants as needed or as you pick.

Geraniums, if they have some summer shade, will continue to bloom nicely, but never with the vigorous growth and intensity of color they had in the North.

Others like zinnias, marigolds, cosmos, and begonias will bloom for several weeks and then start to look seedy. Shearing back will help some, but you will have to be hard hearted now. Yank fading plants out and replace them with something else. Cosmos will drop seeds and renew the planting automatically, but only after a period of adjustment that may be fine in the cutting garden, but not neat or colorful enough for the front door planting. Professionals in places like Busch Gardens renew beds with fresh plants every five or six weeks.

Ageratum, alyssum, petunias, pansies, and nasturtium will continue to bloom until they die of their own accord when the weather no longer suits them.

### Summer

Let trees and shrubs like hibiscus, crape myrtle, and oleander provide much of your color during the summer. But along with them, plant and enjoy summer flowering bulbs like canna, caladium, Aztec lily, butterfly lily, crinum, clivia, moraea, society garlic, spider lily, agapanthus, and gladiolus. Perennials that keep blooming constantly include blue daze, lantana, pentas, many salvias, butterfly weed, and impatiens. Various kinds of daylilies will bloom and often bloom again at their appointed times.

The annuals that bloom all summer include pink or white periwinkle, deep blue torenia (Florida pansy), pink or purple globe amaranth, and portulaca and purslane in many sunshiny shades. Marigolds, zinnias, tithonia, emilia, and cosmos will bloom for a time and then need replacing. Use plenty of coleus, impatiens, torenia, and bromeliads in the shade.

### TIPS ON GROWING ANNUALS AND BIENNIALS

* Buying plants is quicker, easier, and more certain than starting seeds, but some types are not available.

* Start delicate seeds in the clear plastic containers that come from the deli or bakery. Put holes in the bottom. Open and close as needed like a tiny greenhouse.

* Watch plants closely after planting out. Water often but do not drown them. Protect plants from slugs and insects.

* Set out plants when they are available in bloom at the nurseries. Follow the chart on the next page for starting your own plants from seed.

## PLANTING GUIDE FOR ANNUALS AND BIENNIALS (MOST FROM SEED)

| NAME OF PLANT | BEST PLANTING TIME | | | MAIN BLOOM | EASE | EXPOSURE | COLD TOL. |
|---|---|---|---|---|---|---|---|
| | N. FL | C. FL. | S. FL. | | | | |
| alyssum (seeds) | Mar, Aug | Sep-Feb | Oct-Feb | most of year | I | sun or ps | hardy |
| ageratum (seeds) | Mar | Feb-Mar | Nov-Feb | frost--frost | II | sun | tender |
| ammi (seeds) | Feb-Mar | Nov-Feb | Nov-Feb | Apr-Jul | II | sun | tender |
| aster, China (seeds) | Mar | Feb | Feb | May-Jun | II | sun or ps | tender |
| baby's breath (seeds) | Apr | Feb, Nov | Nov-Jan | spring | II | sun or ps | hardy |
| balsam (seeds) | Apr-May | Mar-Apr | Feb-Apr | Apr-Nov | I | sun or ps | tender |
| begonia (plants) | Apr-May | Mar-Apr | Feb-Apr | frost-frost | – | sun or ps | tender |
| browallia (plants) | Apr-May | Mar-Apr | Feb-Apr | frost-frost | – | sun or ps | tender |
| calendula (seeds) | Aug-Sep | Sep-Nov | Oct-Dec | winter-spring | I | sun | hardy |
| calif. poppy (seeds) | Sep-Feb | Nov-Feb | Nov-Feb | Apr-Jun | II | sun | hardy |
| candytuft (seeds) | Sep-Feb | Nov-Feb | Nov-Feb | Apr-Jun | II | sun | hardy |
| celosia (seeds) | Apr-May | Mar | Feb | May-Nov | II | sun | tender |
| cleome (seeds) | Feb-Mar | Feb-Mar | Jan-Feb | Apr-Aug | I | sun | semi-hardy |
| coleus (plants) | Apr-May | Mar-Jun | any time | – | – | ps or shade | tender |
| cornflower (seeds) | Sep | Oct-Nov | Nov-Dec | Feb-Jun | I | sun | hardy |
| cosmos (seeds) | Apr | Mar | Nov-Feb | Apr-Aug | I | sun | tender |
| dianthus (seeds) | Sep | Oct-Nov | Nov-Feb | all year | II | sun | hardy |
| didiscus (seeds) | Apr | Mar | Jan-Feb | Apr-Aug | II | sun | tender |
| dusty miller (plants) | Apr | Mar | Nov-Feb | – | – | sun or ps | hardy |
| emilia (seeds) | fall-spr | fall-spr | fall-spr | Apr-Nov | II | sun | hardy |
| gaillardia (seeds) | Mar | Oct-Dec | Nov-Jan | until frost | I | sun | hardy |
| gazania (seeds) | Sep | Oct-Jan | Nov-Jan | Apr-Sep | IV | sun | semi-hardy |
| globe amaranth (seeds) | Apr | Mar | Feb-Mar | May-Sep | II | sun | tender |
| hollyhock (seeds) | Sep | Oct-Nov | Nov-Dec | Apr | III | sun or ps | hardy |
| larkspur (seeds) | Sep | Oct-Nov | Nov-Dec | Apr-May | III | sun or ps | hardy |
| lobelia (plants) | Apr | Mar-Apr | Dec-Feb | spring, fall | – | sun or ps | tender |
| marigold (seeds) | Apr-Aug | Mar-Sep | all year | until frost | II | sun | tender |
| morning glory (seeds) | Apr | Mar | Dec-Feb | Apr-frost | III | sun or ps | tender |
| nasturtium (seeds) | Apr | Mar | Dec-Feb | Mar-Jun | I | sun or ps | tender |
| nicotiana (plants) | Apr | Mar | Jan-Mar | spr-sum | – | sun or ps | tender |
| phlox (seeds) | Sep-Mar | Oct-Nov | Nov-Jan | spr-sum | II | sun | hardy |
| poppy, shirley (seeds) | Sep, Feb | Nov-Feb | Dec-Feb | spr-frost | III | sun or ps | hardy |
| portulaca (seeds) | Mar-Apr | Mar-Apr | Dec-Mar | spr-frost | I | sun | tender |
| salvia (seeds) | Apr | Mar | Dec-Mar | most of year | II | sun or ps | tender |
| snapdragon (seeds) | Sep | Oct-Mar | Nov-Feb | spr-frost | IV | sun or ps | hardy |
| statice (seeds) | Sep | Oct-Nov | Nov-Dec | Mar-May | II | sun | hardy |
| sunflower (seeds) | Apr | Mar | Nov-Feb | spr-sum | I | sun | tender |
| tithonia (seeds) | Apr | Mar | Nov-Feb | until frost | II | sun | tender |
| torenia (plants) | Apr | Mar | any time | until frost | – | part shade | tender |
| zinnia (seeds) | Apr-May | Mar-Apr | Oct-Apr | until frost | II | sun | tender |

Ease (from seed): I and II =easy; III and IV=harder     ps=partial shade     s=shade     tol.=tolerance

## TIPS ON GROWING PERENNIALS

Don't be surprised if you hear conflicting reports about which perennials are reliably hardy in which parts of Florida. Sun, shade, soil type, moisture, and temperature all come into play. Some are grown like biennials and will not last through summer. All are best planted during moist, mild weather. Here are my suggestions:

### For Northern Florida
achillea, yarrow
anthemis, golden marguerite
*Arctotis lata*, blue-eyed African daisy
babysbreath (*Gypsophila paniculata*)
butterfly weed (*Asclepias tuberosa*)
columbine (*Aquilegia* species)
coreopsis
eustoma (lisianthus)
dahlia
delphinium
feverfew
four o'clock
heliotrope
hosta
iris, bearded
lupine
peony
physostegia (false dragonhead)
poppy, oriental
purple coneflower (*Echinacea purpurea*)
shasta daisy
stoke's aster
viola
violet
yucca

### For Central Florida
agapanthus
anthemis (golden marguerite)
amaryllis
*Arctotis lata*, African daisy
asparagus fern
butterfly weed (*Asclepias tuberosa*)
calla lilies
canna lilies
chrysanthemum
datura
daylily (*Hemerocallis* species)
eustoma (lisianthus)

| | |
|---|---|
| four o'clock | gaillardia |
| gerbera | impatiens |
| physostegia, false dragonhead | |
| shrimp plant | |
| stokes aster | yucca |

### For Southern Florida
amaryllis
anthurium
bird-of-paradise
gaillardia
gerbera, African daisy
gingers
heliconia
impatiens
orchid
salvias
shrimp plant
stokes aster
yucca

### Perennials for shade
*Begonia* species

| | |
|---|---|
| ferns | ginger species |
| impatiens | iris |
| liriope, lily turf | rhoeo, Moses-in-a-boat |
| sansevieria, snake plant | |
| shrimp plant | |
| spiderwort | |
| strawberry geranium | |
| violet, viola | |

### Perennials for wet places
daylily
flat sedge
ginger
ginger-;ily
iris
pickerel weed

### Perennials for sun
blue sage
cacti
century plant
chrysanthemum
daylily
false dragonhead
four o'clock
gerbera
salvia
shasta daisy
shrimp plant
stokes aster
verbena

### Salt-tolerant perennials

| | |
|---|---|
| cacti | century plant |
| daylily | four o'clock |
| gaillardia | sansevieria |
| salvia | vinca |
| violet | yucca |

## TIPS ON GROWING BULBS

Flowers from bulbs, corms, tubers, and rhizomes use these underground structures to help them survive inhospitable times of the year. For some, it is a double challenge of surviving frost damage from winter cold and rot damage from moist, steamy summer heat. Some types of flower bulbs will survive in the ground, unassisted, while others should be dug and stored, then replanted. Keep storage time at a minimum, never longer than nine months. Digging may be for either dry summer storage or for winter warmth. Many bulbs can stay in the ground for several years, until clumps need dividing. In northern Florida, more types should be dug for winter warmth, or else mulched deeply to protect them from frost.

### Bulbs and Roots that Should be Dug and Stored
achimenes
alstroemeria
anemone
calla, dig in north
dahlia
gladiolus
gloriosa lily, dig in north
eucharis, dig in north
lily, true
polianthes
sparaxis
tritonia

gloriosa lily

### Replace Yearly
anemone
iris, dutch
ranunculus

### Bulbs to Leave in the Ground
amaryllis (but mulch or dig in north)
amazon lily, eucharis lily
agapanthus
allium
alstroemeria
blood lily, Haemanthus
caladium
calla, in central and southern zones
crinum lily
crocosmia
eucharis in central and southern zones
freesia
gladiolus
gloriosa lily
hyacinthus
leucojum
lily, in well drained soil
lycoris
narcissus
oxalis
polianthes, only if in well-drained soil
sparaxis
spider lily, *Hymenocallis*
*Tritonia*
*Zephyranthes*, rain lily

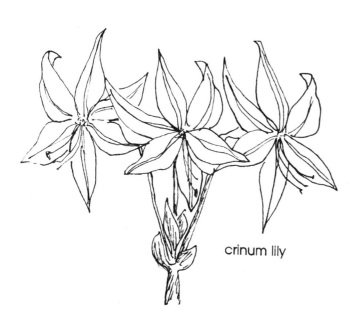

crinum lily

# BULB PLANTING GUIDE FOR FLORIDA

| NAME OF PLANT | *PL. DEPTH | SPACING | BEST PLANTING TIMES | | |
| --- | --- | --- | --- | --- | --- |
| | | | N. FLORIDA | C. FLORIDA | S. FLORIDA |
| Achimenes | .5 in | 2 in | Mar-Apr | Mar | Jan |
| Agapanthus | Cover | 18 in | Mar | Feb | Jan |
| Allium | Varies | Varies | Nov-Jan | Nov | Nov |
| Alstroemeria | 6 in | 24 in | Mar | Feb | Jan |
| Anemone | 2 in | 12 in | Nov-Dec | Nov | Nov |
| Caladium | 2 in | 24-36 in | Mar-May | Feb-Apr | Dec |
| Canna | 3 in | Varies | Mar-Apr | Feb-Apr | Nov-Apr |
| Crinum | Varies | Varies | Nov-Dec | Feb-Apr | Nov-Mar |
| Crocosmia | 5 in | 12 in | Mar-Apr | Feb-Apr | Nov-Mar |
| Dahlia | Cover | 12 in | Mar | Feb-Mar | Nov-Jan |
| Eucharis | Cover | 12-24 in | Apr | Mar | Jan-Feb |
| Freesia | 4 in | 4 in | Oct | Nov | Nov |
| Gladiolus | 5 in | 6 in | Mar-May | Feb-Jun | all |
| Glad (mini) | 4 in | 4 in | Mar-Jun | Feb-Jun | all |
| Gloriosa lily | Cover | 18 in | Mar-Apr | Feb-Mar | Dec-Feb |
| Hippeastrum | Cover | 12 in | Feb-Mar | Nov-Feb | Nov-Feb |
| Hyacinthus | 4 in | 6 in | Nov | Nov | Nov |
| Iris (Dutch) | 4 in | 6 in | Nov | Nov | Nov |
| Ixia | 3 in | 3 in | Mar | Feb | Jan |
| Leucojum | 3 in | 6 in | Nov | Nov | do not plant |
| Lilium | Varies | Varies | Nov | Nov | Nov |
| Lycoris | 3 in | 4-6 in | Nov-Mar | Nov-Jan | Nov |
| Narcissus | 6 in | 6 in | Nov | Nov | Nov |
| Oxalis | 2 in | 4 in | Feb-Mar | Feb | Nov-Feb |
| Polianthes | 2 in | 8 in | May | Feb | Nov |
| Sparaxis | 3 in | 4 in | Nov | Nov | Nov |
| Tritonia | 3iin | 3 in | Mar-May | Feb-Jun | all |
| Zantedeschia | Cover | 12-24 in | Feb-Mar | Nov-Feb | Nov |
| Zephyranthes | 1 in | 3 in | Nov | Nov | Nov |

*PL. DEPTH: Planting depth means cover with this much soil.

## CHAPTER SEVEN
## VEGETABLE GROWING

"It is harder to grow vegetables in the subtropics than almost anyplace else." I read that in Marian Van Atta's newsletter *Living Off the Land* and set out to prove it wrong. After all, I had been growing mainly vegetables for forty years and I know that many of the vegetables grown commercially for the country are grown in Florida. How hard could it be?

Well, Marian was right, and it was in the vegetable garden that I had my greatest setbacks. But it was also in the vegetable garden that I was most determined to succeed. And now I have, to a pleasant extent. I still don't often have the abundance I had in the North, but that is a fact I can live with.

### CULTURE SHOCK

It still is appalling to me that we see very few vegetable gardens in Florida, compared to northern states. This may be because many people try the old ways, fail, and quit before they learn the necessary methods for Florida success.

There seems to be a different attitude here, though, a greater distance from the basic, down-to-earth values that made a vegetable garden part of life for so many of us, no matter where we lived. Coming from Iowa to Tampa involved a great deal of culture shock for me. Seeing so few gardens was one indication. This may be a trend of the times as well.

"Why would you want to grow your own?" one man asked me. You can go out to the fields and buy everything cheap." Sure you can, on certain few days of the year. But time on the road is not the same as a pleasant walk in the garden to pick something for supper.

I prefer to go out into my own yard daily and pick fresh vegetables. If you enjoy the entertainment, exercise, fresh air, and therapy of watching things grow, you can do that, for one crop or another, almost all year in all of Florida.

There are, as I realized after a while, many vegetable gardens hidden behind fences. Also, people plant their vegetables inconspicuously among the flowers and shrubs. I like the idea that gardens in Florida produce smaller amounts over longer times, so less canning and fewer large harvests are necessary. I don't miss the work of canning, but I still miss that feeling of accomplishment that comes from bountiful production.

Five years into Florida living, I know that the difficulties of growing vegetables here are real. Nevertheless I manage to grow a good amount, though nothing like I grew in Iowa. I have written articles about professional growers who seem able to grow almost anything. They are usually willing to use more poisons than most home gardeners are (or should be). Even so, we can emulate their strict adherence to timing, which is the most important ingredient of vegetable growing success in Florida.

### THE UPSIDE DOWN YEAR

Florida vegetable gardens, like school, start in the fall when you can plant the cool season crops like arugula, carrots, lettuce, radishes, celery, beets, cabbage, cauliflower, broccoli, herbs, collards, kale, kohlrabi, mustard, spinach, onions, and turnips. All of these tolerate a touch of frost.

How far north or south you live and the vagaries of each year will dictate whether you start planting these in August or October. In the panhandle and the northern section of the state, plant early because there is a definite, though short, winter when even most of these hardy vegetables will perish.

Here in the Tampa area, they often grow all winter, though an occasional hard freeze means we have to start over again. If we wait until November and the season is kind, we can grow some English peas, but only for a treat, not for filling the freezer. I still am trying short-season corn, but I've had much more success with fall-planted green beans, although they will also be killed by the first hard freeze. Farther south, such crops are less of a gamble. The pros grow tomatoes and if they freeze, they just start over. I keep one or two tomato plants in large pots that can be covered or moved into the garage if necessary.

Spring is the main vegetable gardening season. At that time of year, almost anything grows, but you have to make the most of it because almost everything burns out sometime in June. After that the only crops to grow are heat-lovers: pumpkins, cucuzzi, eggplant, black-eyed peas, cherry tomatoes, sweet potatoes, and okra.

There are vegetables to grow in Florida that I had never heard of. Now our diet includes chayote in the fall and spring, cucuzzi and semi-nole pumpkins through summer, green papayas almost all year, and tampala and Malabar spinach for summer greens. There are still more to try like dasheen and jicama.

**OTHER FACTORS** affect vegetable growth and production. Our veggies are growing when the days are shorter and the sun is lower in the sky, so the plants grow more slowly than they did in the long days of northern summers. This requires patience from us newcomers. Be sure there are at least seven hours of full sun a day for vegetables. But some places too dark for a fall garden will do just fine for a spring one.

Soil needs enriching, seeds need special care, and watering and feeding are necessities. See chapter 3 for more information.

* Varieties are different here. Get the "Vegetable Gardening Guide," Circular 104-0, from the Extension Service and use it or your local seedsman's suggestions for varieties. This means abandoning some old favorites and working with unfamiliar varieties, but that is best at the beginning. After you gain more experience, try a few of your old favorite varieties just to see whether they will work here or not.

* Crops will vary as you learn what grows well for you here and what doesn't. We never ate chayote before, but it grows well for me and we like it very much now. Green papayas replace or accompany squash in all recipes for much of the year. Corn is a special and infrequent treat, but we eat more pumpkin now because I have that from May through February. I never grew arugula before, but we have it all winter now. We grow and eat more fruit here than we ever did before.

* Depth of planting is different. In the North, we planted seed deeper in hot weather to prevent its drying out, so I did that here at first, also. But Barney Yelton, the owner of one of the lushest vegetable gardens I've seen in Florida, planted his seeds no deeper than their longest side, much more shallowly than I had done. Following his guideline seems to work better. Sprinkling often until germination is necessary except in the rainy season, and then slightly deeper planting might prevent washing out.

* Pests and diseases are perhaps more of a problem than in the North. Nematodes can be a serious problem. See chapter 2. Lewis Maxwell's book, *Florida Vegetables*, recommends spraying most crops each week with a combination insecticide and fungicide. I don't and I won't, for I'd rather not chance the effects of eating pesticides. Maybe that is why I haven't been wildly successful, but there's still plenty of great produce growing here! I'll always keep

**THINGS TO SEND FOR:**

**ECHO SEEDLIST.** Educational Concerns for Hunger Organization, 17430 Durrance Road, North Fort Myers, FL 33917. This is an amazing organization. If you come to the area, go on one of the tours of their small but mighty farm, where they develop methods and train Peace Corps workers and missionaries of all faiths to help Third World countries. The tour will make you feel like you can do and grow anything, and the seed list ($1.00) will give you a source of the more unusual vegetables.

**FLORIDA MARKET BULLETIN. To receive this free newsletter, write to MARKET BULLETIN,** Mayo Building, 407 Calhoun Street, Tallahassee, FL 32304. This comes every two weeks and includes articles on Florida agriculture and recipes. There are free ads about plants, seeds, and bulbs available, and U-pick farms, too. If you do not find the plants and seeds you need, you can put an ad in the wanted section.

pesticide use to a bare minimum, even though I am not strictly an organic grower. I don't mind sharing, but if bugs take more than their share, I fight back. Advocates of spraying say such action comes too late, but I can live with that.

For me it is especially important to keep a sharp eye out. Last night I found the telltale damage of a hornworm on a tomato. If I don't find it by today, it will eat the whole plant. They tell me hornworms can eat a whole privet hedge here, so if you find one, squash it even if you hate to. I had not seen hornworm damage since we left Ohio nearly 20 years ago, but recognized it at once. Nothing else eats the whole thing and leaves behind only stubby stems like that.

Spraying the leaves of many plants with a forceful stream of water from the hose on a daily or frequent basis will wash off many pests and disease spores and keep plants in good health. But do it early enough in the day so that the foliage can dry before nightfall. Insecticidal soap controls many pests. *Bacillus thuringiensis* (*Bt*) controls worms in all stages safely. Learn about other new and more natural pesticides available today. Rotenone and pyrethrum are from plants, and biodegrade quickly after use. But they kill bees and other beneficial insects along with the pests.

Choose your own method of pest control. If you use pesticides, start with the safest and use stronger ones only if needed. Always read labels and follow directions carefully. Wear protective clothing during application, then wash it and take a shower.

## HOW TO GROW AND USE SPECIAL CROPS

* **Arugula** or roquette has long, slender, dark green and deeply lobed leaves. Seeds planted in fall will come up in only two days with cabbagelike seedlings, and then grow slowly. But even before Thanksgiving you can add a few leaves to a tossed salad for a peppery pick up. Surprisingly, they are not too strong for a delicious and pretty salad composed of arugula leaves, oranges and/or papayas, and nuts, tossed with a celery seed dressing (or Colonial Salad Dressing from Bob Evans.)

* **Asparagus** is possible though difficult to grow in central Florida, a little easier in northern Florida. Plant at almost any time, the same way you would in the North, either roots or seeds. Plants don't have to go two feet deep, the way people used to do it. A depth of six inches is enough, with 12 to 18 inches between plants. Harvest takes two years from plants, three from seeds. Keep plants moist and well fed. Mulch well to discourage nematodes. If plants don't go dormant on their own, mow them down in early February. Harvest spears in March and April.

The trouble is that it can be quite warm then, and the spears grow quickly and more spindly than one would prefer.

* **Beans** planted in early fall will make a treat for Thanksgiving dinner from central Florida southward, but frost often takes them before they finish bearing. Replant almost at once for a spring crop. Fertilize them well, protect from light frost, and replant every few weeks for continuous crops. If leaves are pale despite feeding, add lime and water well. Beans have more diseases here. Never touch wet plants. Rotate crops to clean soil. Rust-resistant varieties like 'Harvester' have fewer problems. Spray young plants with Maneb (TM). Let older ones bear their crop unsprayed.

Many growers do well with lima beans, but I've had beautiful vines that never yielded a single bean. Too much nitrogen and not enough phosphorus and potassium in the fertilizer, no doubt. Limas like warm weather and can be planted from March through August in northern Florida, March through June and again in September in central, and in all but May through July in the south.

* **Beets** grow fairly well in their own very limited season of September (in northern Florida) or October through February or March in the rest of the state. They must have fertile soil and adequate moisture. Cover during frosts. These are tricky here at best.

* **Broccoli** has done well for me almost from the beginning. Plant seeds or plants or both from August to October and right through January or February. Watch for the same bugs you had up North, aphids and cabbage worms. Feed lightly every two to three weeks, water well, and harvest as ready. After you cut the center cluster, side shoots will continue to develop until the weather gets too hot. If any get away from you and begin to bloom, snap them off at once.

* **Brussels sprouts** grow much the same way and need the same care as cabbage. Plant only in the fall or early winter. This plant does not always do well in Florida, for it needs a long cool season. Remove bottom leaves to encourage bud development. Or cut the center of the top out of the plant when it is tall enough. Insects can be a problem and warm weather may result in puffy rather than solid little heads.

* **Cabbage** has always done well for me here as long as I grow it in cool weather. The red ones are especially attractive in the garden and in the salad. Sow from September through January or February. Cabbage is a heavy feeder, so fertilize often. It is a cabbageworm's delight, but no more difficult in Florida during the winter than elsewhere in summer. It will survive light freezes. One neighbor remarked with surprise that my cabbage looked "real, just like in the grocery store." Usually insects are not too pesky, but be ready with *Bt* if the worms attack.

* **Carrots** are grown much the same as beets, but are a little easier. I've had fairly decent carrots from the first. Again, grow only during the cooler months and be sure to harvest before summer, or some pest will do it for you. An easy way to grow carrots that need no thinning is to make a wide row and sprinkle a few seeds together at one-foot intervals along the row. The little clumps have room to spread out because of the spaces between them.

* **Celery** does remarkably well here. A dozen plants or less, planted six inches apart in a little plot of well-enriched soil near the hose, will produce plenty for a family. Plant in fall or earliest spring because it likes cool weather. I harvest side stalks as needed until summer comes. Then I harvest the whole plant before the summer heat. Blend the leaves with a little water, freeze in ice cube trays, and package in bags for adding to soups or stews. Or dry them. Chop and freeze the stems for cooked dishes. Keep celery for weeks in the hydrator drawer of the refrigerator for eating fresh.

Homegrown celery is greener and thinner, but more nutritious and flavorful than the blanched product in the grocery. You can blanch your homegrown celery by hilling up with soil or surrounding with tarpaper rings to keep out the light, but it seems to me more trouble than it is worth. You may wish to store some celery seed in the freezer (for good germination) because it is not always possible to buy plants or seeds when you want them.

* **Chinese cabbage** grows easily during the cool weather. Harvest while young and tender and before the heat turns it bitter.

* **Collards** need the same care as cabbage and do very well in Florida's cool months. Sow from August through April.

* **Cauliflower** has done well for me from the first winter. Treat like cabbage, but pin up the leaves with snap clothespins to cover forming heads and keep them white. Check the seed catalog for interesting new types.

* **Corn** needs well-enriched soil, plenty of sun, heavy feeding, and lots of water. It can endure only a little water stress. Plant in blocks of four rows for best pollination. Corn can be transplanted, even purchased in market packs here, and these do well. Feed every two to three weeks. Do not crowd. Writer Lewis Maxwell plants on his birthday in late July for a fall crop. Most of the market growers plant only in the spring. There is nothing I like better than seeing the tiny shoots piercing the ground. Much of mine comes to little more, but occasionally I get a crop of almost northern quality. Keep trying.

But also buy ripe corn from the markets during the season and enjoy it for the few weeks it is available. Silver Queen is a favored crop here, but we think the yellow corn like 'Bonanza' tastes better. Be aware that what is sold in the markets in the summer was probably grown in your northern home state and shipped. Market people have told me proudly on a Saturday, "That is real fresh. It just came in on Thursday."

* **Cucumbers** are supposed to be easy and often grow by the fieldful, but I have had trouble with them. Plant suggested varieties such as 'Poinsett,' 'Sprint,' 'Spacemaster,' 'Galaxy,' or 'SMR 18.' These are most resistant to mildew and other diseases. Our shortage of bees can reduce pollination. Planting some of two varieties, one with male flowers, will help. Keep vines mulched and well watered, and watch carefully for insects.

* **Eggplant** likes hot weather and does very well here. But somehow my first success, the best eggplant production of my life, took a few years to repeat. Some people get plants to thrive and produce for several years, without frost killing them. The Japanese varieties that produce small, oblong fruit seem to get less bitter than standard types. Also try white, egg-shaped 'Albino' and 'White Beauty.' They have a sweet, mild flavor and are ornamental besides. Feed every two to three weeks until plants begin to bloom, every three or four weeks after that. Pick the fruit while it is still shiny.

* **Herbs.** The herbs I planted during my first fall did so well all winter that I thought they were easy here. Then summer came and wiped some out.

Herbs that will live over summer in central Florida include anise hyssop, aloe, ajuga, basil, butterfly weed, chicory, comfrey, dandelion, elderberry, eucalyptus, ginger, goldenrod, lemon grass, some mints, moneywort, passion flower, periwinkle, rosemary, certain sages, and a coleus variety that tastes like oregano.

Nasturtiums, chives, and lemon balm survive the heat if moved into deep shade, and perhaps several more species will do this as well. Others like parsley, savory, leek, coriander, borage, cress, dill, fennel, and marjoram are best restarted from seeds or new plants in the fall.

The dandelions I brought down, among guffaws from my northern friends, from a spring trip to Ohio, grow just fine but tend to be too bitter to eat most of the time. The blooms come and go so quickly in the heat that they are seldom seen, but I like to see a few for old time's sake. The comfrey does not grow as tall or lush, and only blooms rarely. I am still experimenting, but many herbs grow well in the poor soil or in containers and are as rewarding here as elsewhere. We just have to work around summer for those that can't take the heat and humidity, protect tender types from winter freezes, and sometimes be satisfied with less vigorous growth.

Nasturtiums that cover the fence and bloom abundantly from Thanksgiving to June weigh nicely in the balance and we enjoy them in colorful, tasty salads.

If you are a herb grower, be sure to subscribe to Kay Cude's newsletter (see page 9).

* **Lettuce** does moderately well from early fall to mid-spring. It thrives in mid-winter where and when the frosts are light. Leaf and bibb types do best but head lettuces are possible for the skilled or determined. For the warmer part of the year, forget lettuce and plant other greens like tampala or Malabar spinach. These like the summer and can be harvested, with the right growing conditions, in only five or six weeks.

* **Kale** and kohlrabi grow easily in cool weather, much the same as cabbage but with a somewhat shorter season.

* **Melons** (cantaloupe, watermelon, honeydew, and others) are grown commercially in Florida in the spring and are possible in home gardens with a little extra care. Plant from February to April, after danger of frost passes, and again in August and September for southern Florida only. Mulch and treat weekly with *Bt* or Sevin to control pickleworms. Check fragrance and color for ripeness. Stems do not slip as easily in Florida, so don't depend on that to indicate ripeness for you. For the best flavor, melons need sun and enough but not too much water. If you don't have space to grow your own, buy local melons from fruit stands in May and June. I've gotten delicious big cantaloupes for 75 cents each.

* **Mustard** or mustard spinach is a natural for Florida gardens, for it has a long season of weather tolerance. Sow from September right through March in all sections of the state. Mustard seed can germinate almost overnight. Speed of growth depends on the season. Keep it cut back by harvesting often, to within two inches of the ground. Feed every two or three weeks. Keep moist, and cover during all but light frosts.

Cook it like spinach. My family would not touch it even in salads, but they love it in green noodles. Wash and blend the mustard with eggs for noodle recipes, with milk or tomato juice for meat loaf, or with as little water as possible and freeze it like celery leaves for seasoning, or for other recipes that call for spinach.

* **Okra** also likes the summer, but it needs continuous supplies of water and fertilizer to thrive. It is particularly susceptible to nematodes. If you grow okra, pick it daily to keep the pods from developing past the small and tender stage. Let a few escape at the end of the season to use in dried arrangements or wreaths, but constant picking is necessary to keep the plants producing. If you have stinkbugs, oval, greenish brown sucking insects that stink if touched (but you wouldn't want to!) use malathion before the plants flower or the pods may be deformed.

Wash and slice the pods crosswise, toss them in a bowl with cornmeal, and pan-fry in butter for an easy and delicious introduction to a favorite Southern vegetable. Some people like steamed or pickled okra, and almost everyone likes okra in gumbo.

* **Onions** grow large and lush at the ends of the rows in strawberry fields when the berries ripen, a hint of their growing time. Sets and plants are available at garden stores. Onions are fairly easy, but not quite the carefree crop they were up north. Without plenty of water and feeding, they will come to nothing. With, they will grow as large as baseballs and as sweet as Georgia's Vidalias, because of the climate. Plant seeds or transplants of Florida varieties from September to November in southern and central Florida, from September to December in northern Florida. Sets will produce good scallions, not large bulbs. Feed every three or four weeks. Onions and their relatives tolerate light freezes.

Gary Staley of Brandon, Florida grows thriving rows of Texas Granex red and white onions that looked very large even the year he only planted them from plants in January. "The best time to plant onions is when you plant strawberries," he says. "In Florida you must plant short day onions. The long day kinds, including onions from sets and all kinds of garlic, will never form bulbs here."

* **Peanuts** should be sown in early spring only, and make a fascinating garden project for children. Be sure the pH of your soil is slightly acid. Plant shelled seeds with the brown covering intact if possible. Feed well with low-nitrogen fertilizer and add calcium and gypsum when flowering begins. You may need to spray with Bravo(TM), Dithan M-45(TM), or copper to control leaf spot. Follow label directions. Plants can also be damaged by frost or by nematodes. Dig the vines when pods seem mature. Boiled peanuts make a favorite dish here. Cook them as soon as you dig them. Allow peanuts for roasting to dry out in the sun first.

* **Peas** of the English and sugar snap type are not at home in Florida, but you can grow them during cooler months with careful timing. Sow in October through February in central and southern Florida, January through March in northern Florida. Plants but not blossoms will tolerate light freezes. Because there will be no large pea harvests like the 50 quarts a year we used to freeze, the sugar snaps (eat the whole pod) are the most practical. **Southern peas**, on the other hand, thrive through the summer and are an excellent cover crop even if you don't harvest and eat them. But frequent harvests are necessary if you want continuous production.

* **Peppers**, especially the sweet bell types, will grow and sometimes live for several years if protected from frost. They do well either in pots, or in the garden. Hot peppers are ornamental in flower beds. Chile and exotic peppers do well because of the long growing season. More and more kinds are available. Ancho chiles are moderately hot, and great for stuffing. Yellow, orange, red, and brown bell peppers have time to ripen to their full coloration.

Feed plants every three weeks and stake them if necessary. Mulch and keep soil moist. Leaf spot disease in the humid months should respond to a copper spray or Maneb. Peppers produce three to four crops a year rather than continuously, so freeze the extras . I like to grow one or two of the hot, ornamental kind, too.

For homemade pest repellant, put a few of the hot little peppers into the blender with a quart of water, and a garlic clove for extra pungency. A spoonful of salad oil helps the concoction stick. Blend, let sit, then strain and spray on garden plants. Few insects or squirrels like the taste.

* **Potatoes**, regular (white or red) can be grown in Florida, but they do better the farther north you live in the state. Plant them in January, February, or March in northern Florida. January and February are best in central Florida, September to December in southern Florida. Feed well or they will be the size of marbles.

Sweet potatoes and yams like the heat and humidity and are perennial in Florida. They will make quite a good groundcover. Start them by planting tubers or pieces that have begun to sprout. Those from the grocery have been treated to prevent their sprouting, but you can rough up their outer coating with a little soap and water and steel wool and get them to grow for you anyway. Or you can buy starter plants of named varieties at the garden store. If soil is too rich in nitrogen, sweet potatoes can be all leaf and no root. Mulch well to prevent nematode damage and hill up with soil for more production.

* **Pumpkins** are a fine example of the necessity for planting the right variety. Get Seminole pumpkins (Southern Seeds has these) or calabaza squash. I planted them once and had big squashes to give away for five months of the summer. And since then, new plants volunteer every year. Let them take over the garden in the summer when little else will grow and learn from the Cubans the many ways to cook both of these. Some will turn a fine tan and we make our Jack-o-lanterns from these. I cook and freeze whole ones at a time and have a constant supply for pumpkin bread, muffins, or cake. Cook and serve them almost any way you would sweet potatoes. You can also cook the vine tips and young leaves like spinach or in stir-fry. And roast the seeds as you would almonds, with butter and salt, for a delicious snack.

* **Radishes** have a short season, but at last I had almost a ground cover of them with big sweet bulbs from sowings among the peas in November. They withstand light freezes and can be sown at frequent intervals from September to March in northern Florida, from October or November to March in central and southern Florida. Winter radishes don't necessarily need winter. Sow them in September in northern Florida, October through December in central and southern Florida. Feed lightly every three or four weeks.

* **Spinach** is possible, like beets, for a short season in the winter when and where conditions cooperate. It is easiest in northern Florida, where a September sowing is best. Here in central Florida, Barney Yelton has a wide row that would make any northern gardener proud. Market gardeners in Ruskin, Florida grow it for the grocery stores. Plant in October or November. Other greens like collards and kale have a longer season. Use them in the same recipes and don't mention the difference to your family.

* **Squash** is a variable crop here. Most of the northern ones can be grown if you employ pinpoint timing. Among them, the scallop "Patty

Pan" has done best for me. Cucuzzi is a delicious and dependable substitute for zucchini in the summer if you give it the water, feeding, and support it needs. But pick it quickly or it gets to be as large and hard as a baseball bat. For much of the year, we use green papayas and chayotes in squash recipes. Our favorite is a scalloped casserole with herbed bread crumbs, cream of chicken soup, and sour cream or cream cheese mixed with the cooked squash and then baked.

* **Swiss chard**, especially rhubarb chard, was one of my favorite crops up north, though I used it mostly as an ornamental and in flower arranging. It has not done well for me here, but the experts agree that it is possible to grow chard here, even year-round, with rich soil and a constant supply of moisture. My next try will be in the containers with some of my herbs.

* **Tomatoes** grow nicely here until frost or summer kills the plants. Some of the cherry types will survive most of the summer. However, a horde of pests may arrive to eat them before you do.

Marian Van Atta recommends the ring method of growing, with a circle of concrete-reinforcing wire about four feet in diameter and also in height. Make the ring a compost pile with leaves and grass clippings. Put four or five tomato plants around the edge and train them up through the wires. My own best tomatoes have been those grown in pots, almost hydroponically considering the soil, with tomato rings for support. Lots of feeding and watering is needed for these. With the plants up off the ground, the bugs have a harder time finding them. When the sun moves, so do the plants. In case of frost, several can come into the garage. Half a dozen of these potted tomato plants can supply a family.

* **Turnips** and other root crops are not difficult if you plant them in the fall or early spring. Most will tolerate frost and light freezes. Prepare soil well, add fertilizer before planting, and feed again every two to three weeks. Eat the tops of turnips as well. Rutabagas need cool temperatures to grow large. *Bt* will keep cutworms from making your seedlings disappear. Harvest when mature and refrigerate in a plastic bag. Insects move in if they stay in the ground too long.

For the best times to plant vegetables in your part of Florida, check the chart on the next page.

## PLANTING TIMES FOR FLORIDA VEGETABLES

| VEGETABLE | Jan | Feb | Mar | Apr | May | Jun | Jul | Aug | Sep | Oct | Nov | Dec |
|---|---|---|---|---|---|---|---|---|---|---|---|---|
| asparagus | N C | N C | N C | N C | N C | N C | N C | N C | N C | N C | N C | N C |
| bean, lima | S | S | NC S | NCS | N C | N C | N | N S | C S | S | S | S |
| bean, snap | S | S | NCS | NCS | C | | | N | NCS | C S | S | S |
| beets | NCS | NCS | NC | | | | | | N | NCS | NCS | NCS |
| broccoli | NCS | N | | | | | | NC | NCS | NCS | NCS | NCS |
| brussels sprouts* | | | | | | | | | N | NC | NCS | NCS |
| cabbage* | NCS | N | | | | | | | NCS | NCS | NCS | NCS |
| cab., Chinese | NCS | | | | | | | | | NC | NCS | NCS |
| cantaloupe | | S | NCS | NC | | | | S | S | | | |
| carrots | NCS | NCS | NC | | | | | | N | NCS | NCS | NCS |
| cauliflower* | NCS | N | | | | | | N | N | NCS | CS | CS |
| celery* | NCS | NC | N | | | | | | C | C | CS | CS |
| collards | CS | NCS | NC | C | | | | N | NCS | NCS | NCS | NCS |
| corn, sweet | S | CS | NCS | N | | | N | NCS | CS | S | S | S |
| cucumbers | S | NCS | NCS | N | | | | NC | NCS | S | S | S |
| eggplant | S | NCS | NC | N | N | N | N | CS | CS | S | | S |
| endive | CS | NC | N | | | | | | NCS | S | S | S |
| kale | NCS | NC | | | | | | | | NC | NCS | NCS |
| kohlrabi | S | CS | NC | N | | | | | | NC | NCS | S |
| lettuce | CS | CS | NC | N | | | | | NCS | CS | CS | CS |
| mustard | NCS | NCS | NCS | | | | | | NCS | NCS | NCS | NCS |
| okra | | S | NCS | NCS | NCS | NC | NC | CS | S | | | |
| onions | | | | | | | | | NCS | NCS | NCS | NC |
| parsley | CS | N | N | | | | | | S | CS | CS | CS |
| peanuts | | S | NCS | NC | N | | | | | | | |
| peas, English | NCS | NCS | N | | | | | | | CS | CS | CS |
| peas, southern | S | S | NCS | NCS | NC | NC | NC | NCS | CS | S | S | S |
| peppers* | S | S | NCS | NCS | | | N | NCS | CS | S | S | S |
| potatoes, reg. | NS | NC | N | | | | | | CS | CS | S | S |
| potatoes, swt. | | S | NCS | NCS | NCS | NCS | CS | | | | | |
| pumpkin | S | S | NC | NC | | | NCS | NCS | S | | | |
| radishes | NCS | NCS | NCS | | | | | | N | NC | NCS | NCS |
| rhubarb | N | N | N | N | N | N | N | NCS | NCS | NCS | N | N |
| spinach | S | | | | | | | | | NCS | NCS | CS |
| spin., Malabar | | S | CS | NCS | NCS | NCS | NCS | NCS | CS | | | |
| squash, summer | S | S | NCS | N | | | | NC | NCS | S | | |
| squash, winter | S | S | NC | | | | | C | | | | |
| strawberries* | | | | | | | | | NC | NCS | S | |
| swiss chard | NCS | NCS | NCS | | | | | | NCS | NCS | NCS | NCS |
| tampala | | S | CS | NCS | NCS | NCS | NCS | NCS | CS | | | |
| tomatoes | S | S | NCS | N | | | | NCS | CS | S | S | S |
| turnips | NCS | NCS | NC | N | | | | N | NC | NCS | CS | S |
| watermelon | S | CS | NCS | N | | | N | NCS | S | | | |

* =plants (not seeds)    N=northern, C=central, S=southern Florida

# CHAPTER EIGHT
## WONDERFUL FLORIDA FRUITS

Fruits grow really well in Florida, and there are many kinds you can choose. Growing fruit in Florida is as easy and natural as it is fun and rewarding. If you ever wished you'd have as much fruit as vegetable production from your yard, that wish could soon come true. The wide range of possibilities includes both familiar and exotic varieties.

Different parts of the state have different climates, and there are also annual fluctuations. This variability is an advantage as well as a disadvantage. If it is cold, certain fruits like apples, peaches, pears, and plums do better, for they like chilling in winter. If the winter is warm, citrus and tropical fruits will bear abundantly. Plant fruit from each group, and you will always have something, no matter what kind of weather you get.

### FIRST LESSONS
Here is information on growing fruit that I wish I had known when I first arrived in Florida:

* Planting trees here is not the investment in time that it is in the North. Trees grow quickly and some produce within the first year. Therefore, if a tree freezes out every four or five years and has to be replaced, it may still be well worth the effort and expense of planting it.

* Most fruit trees in Florida are natural dwarfs or can be pruned that way. The dwarf varieties that were so important in the North are irrelevant here.

* Florida growers can use very few of the fruit selections from general mail order catalogs that are sent all over the country. Buy from local nurseries or Florida-based specialists who will have the varieties that are hardy here. Tree and plant sales sponsored by the Rare Fruit Council International (RFCI) are great for buying fruit trees of all kinds. You'll also find recipes, information, and fellowship with other fruit growers.

I have enjoyed my membership in this group tremendously. There are chapters in several areas.

* Many fruit trees, especially citrus, are so ornamental that edible landscaping is easy. But keep in mind the results of frosts. I plant all clumps of bananas in the back yard, out of direct view from any window, because they look bad during almost any winter and terrible after a frost. However, they come back from the roots and are a lovely, lush, tropical accent from April until cold weather the next winter. So I keep one clump close enough to the living room windows to cast delightful shadows and give me the music of their large leaves rustling in the breeze.

* Citrus are among the easiest of fruits to grow in Florida. Except for the frost worry, they have few problems as dooryard trees. Choose kinds and varieties that are hardy for your area. Given ample water and fertilizer, they will soon bear plenty of fruit for family and friends. The blossoms perfume the air for an entire month in spring.

However, there are many stringent and ever-changing laws to protect the citrus industry. For a time, no homegrown citrus fruit could be shipped out of the state. That has lately changed, but is subject to change again at the first sign of disease or pest problems for the industry. When you buy a citrus tree, usually you have to register that fact, and inspectors may come to your yard to check your plants for pests and diseases.

"Don't mulch citrus trees," my fruit growing friends told me, so I hardly ever did except when the grass got very threatening. It took me years to learn that the trees are susceptible to foot rot and need free air circulation and good water drainage around the root area, especially near the trunk. Cultivate carefully, but do not mulch, as a rule. If it is a choice between mulch or weeds, mulch is better, but keep it away from the trunk and pull it back as soon as it kills the weeds.

## WILL MY FAMILY LIKE GRUMICHAMA? OR WHATEVER?

Of course, plant your favorite fruits first and buy varieties recommended by a friend or a book. You can also buy and taste exotic kinds of fruit from the grocery to see whether you should plant them. Don't let this prejudice you too much, however. The first carambolas I bought, at a surprisingly high price, did not taste all that good. But when I got tree-ripened ones, they were delicious. I had to learn that carambolas, mangoes, papayas, and many other Florida fruits vary in taste from plant to plant and even from the same plant at different times. Ripeness and freshness affect flavor, too, as with any fruit. Try exotic new fruits along with your favorites. Whatever you plant, your family will like it at once or learn to like it soon, for you will be harvesting each kind at its peak.

## HOW SHOULD I START?

The county agricultural extensive service is a great help with both bulletins and advice. To start, ask which days the volunteers are there if you'd rather talk to them than bother the experts. On your first trip to the library or book store, get Lewis Maxwell's small book, *Florida Fruit,* or Marian Van Atta's *Growing and using Exotic Foods.* You will use either one for years.

Then, as your interest grows, join the nearest chapter of Rare Fruit Council International. I went to their annual tree sale back when I was too green to know which questions to ask or plants to buy. And the last thing I thought I wanted was to join any group. Months later, I got out their flyer to look at the list of plants one can grow in our area. Then I noticed that, at the next plant sale, members get a discount that would more than cover my dues. The meeting date and place happen to be convenient for me, but many members never go to meetings, instead

they read the newsletter's encapsulation of each speaker's talk.

Our Tampa group has friendly people, a free seed and sometimes a free plant exchange, a delicious spread of food where you can taste fruit and gather recipes, and a plant auction and raffle from which many of my own trees have come. At first much of the talk at meetings went over my head, but soon I began to understand more of it. I always come home feeling like I can do anything. My "fruit friends" are some of my favorite people.

Mostly, you will learn by growing and have so much fun doing it that the time will fly. Whatever you grow will help you learn more about growing everything else, and eventually everything you learned before coming to Florida will stand you in good stead as well. You are really not starting from scratch, just taking a sharp bend in the road.

## SHOULD I BUY A SEEDLING TREE OR A GRAFTED ONE?

If you win one at a fruit meeting, or are given one, accept either a seedling or grafted tree happily. If your space is limited, leave the seedling in the pot until you check on bearing time in *Florida Fruit* or a similar book.

Some trees, like carambola, have been known to bear in as little as 24 months from seed. Others, like avocado and mango, will take up to ten years to bloom from seed, but only a year or two from grafted stock. All seedlings are surprises. Grafted fruit will have the same flavor, fruiting time, and such as the parent plant. So for most purposes, grafted is better, but sometimes it does not matter. Eventually you may want to learn to graft so you can try many varieties on a few trees. Then you can keep the ones that are superior and discard the others.

## HOW BIG A TREE SHOULD I BUY?

How big a tree can you transport home? If you don't have an orange tree in your yard, what price would you put on getting a crop next year instead of three years from now?

The difference in price between a larger and a smaller tree can seem less important if you consider how much you'll enjoy getting ripe oranges right away. I wished, after I'd bought the gallon pot size, that I'd invested in the three gal-

lon pot size for at least one of the orange trees and one of the grapefruits. Keep in mind that kum-quats and calamon-dins bear on smaller, younger trees or shrubs. Those al-ready large enough to bear these fruits are not expensive.

After a few years, it was a convenience to me to buy second varieties in small sizes so that I could afford more, get more in the car, dig smaller holes, and cover the plants more easily during frosty nights. But first I wanted to have some trees that were large enough to produce fruit. Now, in my sixth year here, I have 42 different kinds of fruit. Some of the plants are still tiny, but about half have bloomed and a third have borne at least a sample crop. Some, like my yellow plum, have been producing for three years. And this year, for the first time in my life, I have had some fruit to pick and eat almost every day all year.

You can plant potted trees and shrubs at any season of the year, so you can start your fruit growing before you get your unpacking finished. A trip to a reputable nursery, and in Florida there are almost as many of them as there are banks, is a good morale booster during your settling in time. Once you get your new plants home, you don't necessarily have to hurry to plant them. You will find a new way of growing them in containers here that will far surpass all your initial prejudices.

## SOME FRUIT FAVORITES

I saw **elderberries** blooming almost all year in the wild. I had tried a few cuttings and failed when I finally recognized a few of the "weeds" in my yard as elderberries, my old friends from the ditches of Ohio. I now have several bushes growing, blooming, and fruiting. I use both the bloom and the unripe berries in flower arranging, the ripe berries for pies and wine, and the flowers for herbal cosmetics and teas. I find the large shrubs quite attractive, but if you don't, you can tuck them into the back corners. Or you can seek out the ornamental cultivar with white and green variegated leaves.

Elderberries love water and will grow in low places. You often see them as ten-foot shrubs along the roadside, bearing huge, flat umbels of white flowers or purple berries.

**Rhubarb** may be grown in Florida, but it must be grown like an annual. It will never match what you had farther north, but half a dozen pampered plants will produce a few pies and batches of jelly before they perish in the summer heat. I have successfully dug and frozen roots over the summer and replanted them in fall.

**Strawberries** also grow like annuals in Florida. Whether to get everbearers or June bearers is not a consideration here. Florida varieties like 'Florida 90,' 'Tioga,' 'Dover,' and 'Douglas' can bear from December into June if well fed, watered, and protected from frost. And even the frost will kill only the blossoms, not the plant. Plants will begin to bear again in about six weeks. It is fun to have a few around the house to watch and use to perk up fruit salads. If you want to fill your freezer, hit the fields in the spring as soon as the ads for three or four quarts

for a dollar, pick-them-yourself, appear in the classified ad section. They don't take long to pick. I just wash, hull, and freeze, and then use them all year long.

One of my favorite trees is a yellow **plum**. It is very hardy and will bloom all winter if the weather is mild. At first I lost most of the fruit to insects as it ripened. But now I know to pick a bowlful every day of the ripest or just-dropped

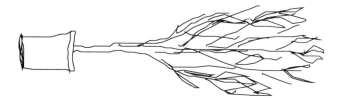

plums. Whatever we don't eat is cut up, seeded and frozen before the next picking. These are good in winter desserts. But we have fresh, sweet plums as delicious as any in the North, and we have them for weeks in May and June. Figs and other fruits also must be picked daily, so put them near the house or along your daily path.

## GROWING FRUIT IN CONTAINERS

In Florida, growing plants in containers outdoors is not at all like growing houseplants indoors in the North. There the atmosphere was completely unnatural. Outdoors here there is plenty of light and humidity. You still have to add water and fertilizer, but you have to do that for in-ground plants as well. Outdoors you can water with a hose instead of worrying about dripping on the furniture.

The insects that were so uncontrollable in a heated house are not nearly as difficult outdoors. You have natural predators to help. The plants are far enough off the ground to discourage some pests. You can easily wash them off with water from the hose, with or without using a hose-end sprayer filled with a mix of detergent and water.

The only disadvantage to container growing is the eventual size of pot you will need to accomodate the ever-growing plants, and the frequent necessity of shifting them into larger pots. However, it will take some time before they grow large enough to need extremely large pots. In the months ahead, you can figure out whether to continue the plants on in pots, or to plant them in the ground.

But in the meantime, you can grow more plants in less space in containers. You can take better care of them if they are together. You can move them from shade or partial shade to more

sun as you become increasingly aware of the changing shadow patterns with the different seasons. You can put your calamondin orange tree by the door where you'll catch its fragrance while it blooms, and its color when it is bearing. And when something else you have looks better, you can interchange the two.

Turn a large, container-grown tree on its side and cover it with a blanket to protect it from frost. Later, when immediate danger of frost is past, set it back up.

Best of all, you can bring a container into the house or garage if a frost comes, and thus save a plant you might have lost in the ground. Even if it is too big to move indoors, you can turn the pot onto its side and cover a ten-foot tree with leaves or a blanket much more easily than if it is vertical. I roll my avocado up close to the above-ground pool.

Many of my "fruit friends" grow some trees in containers permanently because they would not survive our frosts here otherwise. One man planted two fruit trees of the same size and species, one in the ground and one in a container. The one in the container bore fruit first.

The containers themselves can be expensive. Save any large pots you empty or see left out for trash pickup. Some garden centers will let you have their used pots either free or for a small sum: they cannot afford the time it would take to wash them.

One fruit society member came to the rescue by selling recycled plastic barrels he had gotten from work. He had cut them in half, put drainage holes in the bottom, and handle holes in the top. Mine are 21 inches across the top and 16 inches deep, large enough to keep a small tree happy well into its fruit-producing days. He sold them for $2.50 apiece, a real bargain for us and a profit for him. They are heavy to move and they gobble up the soil, though.

Another advantage to growing fruit in containers is that you can fill them with plenty of good soil, making a friendlier environment for the roots than they would find in the ground.

Armondo Mendez, an excellent fruit grower, picks fresh fruit from a fairly small yard in Tampa every day of the year. When he plants a tree in the ground he digs a large hole and adds one 40-pound bag of treated manure and two 40-pound bags of topsoil. But it takes that much or more to fill a large container.

To make the containers lighter when filled, and the medium more water-retentive, use up to one third good organic matter. Sphagnum peat moss is one of the best choices because it does not break down and disappear as quickly as compost. It is also sterile. But it does not add any nutrients, so feel free to use as much compost or well-rotted manure as you have. Some experts find that using perlite for up to a third of the organic third is helpful for aeration. Perlite and vermiculite have virtually no weight themselves; they are only as heavy as the water they hold. Most garden stores sell them by the small bagful, but if you ask, you can order the four-cubic-foot size, which is much more economical.

Placing mulch on the top of your containers will hold in the moisture and improve appearance. You can also grow flowers, herbs, or salad vegetables around the base of the large fruit tree, in its large pot.

To make the best use of his limited space, Armando Mendez has about half of his fruit in containers, the rest in the ground. The plants in his containers sit among and between the younger trees until they spread and need more

room. The containers dry out quickly, and force him to get around with the hose every few days, so none of the plants, in ground or in container, get too dry. He has better control during frost and grows and fruits some plants, like his black sapote (chocolate pudding fruit ) that would never survive in the ground. His compact yard is well landscaped largely with deliciously productive edible plants, and is quite unique.

There is not much grass area left in the Mendez yard, none at all on the sides or in back. But when asked which took more time and work, the grass or the fruit, Armando answered without hesitation, "The grass."

**papaya**

## PROTECTING FRUIT FROM FROSTS

Frosts are a fact of Florida life in almost all areas. All of Florida is too warm for most of the fruits we grew up North, though there are some varieties of apples, peaches, blueberries, and grapes, the ones that need the fewest chilling hours to bloom and fruit, that will grow here. On the other hand, we are too far north to grow truly tropical fruits without extra help during those occasional frosts. So most of us fruit growers plant some trees for a tropical and some  for a temperate climate, so we are sure to have something to harvest even in an abnormally cold or warm year. But without advice, it would be all too easy for a newcomer to conclude that nothing will grow here!

Concentrate on planting types of fruit that will grow with no frost protection in your area. Because our climate is so variable, most fruit growers can't resist the challenge of trying borderline plants. "I can grow anything along the south side of my house," says one fruit grower. "The trouble is, I've run out of south side."

Check for cold hardiness before you buy or plant any fruit trees, and plant them accordingly. Plant the ones that are hardy anywhere out in the yard wherever there is enough sun, ones that are borderline in protected spots or where you can cover them easily, and tender ones in containers so you can move them inside as needed.

A few fruit growers have greenhouses, very tall ones so small trees can go inside. My friend Louis Zohrer in Spring Hill, Florida, has a

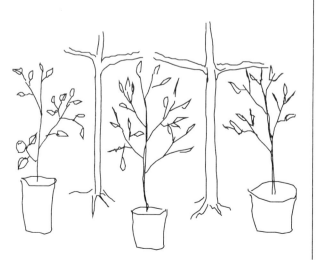

framework of PVC pipe over his grapefruit tree and covers that with a secondhand parachute during frosts. He bought the parachute at an army surplus store for $75 and has used it for years. He also puts a heater under the branches. After the Christmas freeze of 1989, he lost some leaves, but still picked 18 bushels of grapefruit. Most trees bear half that at best.

Fruit trees tend to grow more hardy as they mature, so it is often possible to cover them during frosts for the first several winters and have them survive on their own after that.

Many fruits grow and bear well for several years, are killed back by a severe frost, and come back from the roots to bear again in a few months, for bananas, or in a few years, for citrus. But if they are grafted plants and come back from the roots below the graft, you could have a very different fruit. That is why it pays to hill tender plants with soil to above the graft point before frost. You often see this done in commercial groves.

> Heap soil or mulch above graft.

I finally learned that when the bananas are frozen back, it is best to leave the sad looking corpses just as they are to protect the heart until all danger of frost is past. Then cut them back, not to the ground, but as high up as you can reach. Cut the outer rim, going lower and lower if necessary, until you find green growth at the center. Let the plant restart from there and you'll get blooms much sooner.

My first papayas hung green for months, and I did not know to take them in, green or not, before the Christmas freeze. They were pulp by the next morning. Now I pick and use the green papayas all year long, and before a freeze I pick from a boxful to the entire crop, according to the forecast.

**WHAT IF I GET TOO MUCH?**

You will be amazed at the amount of fruit your family can use if they pick and eat it fresh. My banana plants froze to the ground for the first two winters, but a Plant City grower assured me that his nearly always froze, yet always came back and produced bananas. The winter of '90-'91 was a mild one, and the banana bloom that opened on Christmas day ripened in mid-May. That year we had 12 bunches of bananas, prob-

ably between 150 and 200 pounds altogether, and not more than one pound went to waste. In fact, not more than ten pounds made it to the freezer. They were so delicious, sweeter and tastier than any we'd ever bought, that we just ate them up.

One friend with 45 persimmon trees in his yard says simply, "We have plenty of friends who will be glad to eat the ones we can't."

Should you ever get to the wonderful point of overabundance, you could easily sell the extra. It is amazing how few people take advantage of the climate to grow citrus trees. And many years there are ads in the paper asking to buy and harvest fruit from as few as ten orange trees from yards that once were groves.

But it is easy to make preserves, fruit leather, and special treats with all the fruit. Marian Van Atta's book, *Growing and Using Exotic Foods,* is filled with growing instructions and recipes, including a basic wine recipe Marian and Jack Van Atta have used with great success with most fruits. Only their sea grape batch turned to vinegar -- which Marian then used in chutney.

Here are recipes my family loves:
**Fruit slush (for any fruit)**. After our first spring of picking many quarts from the strawberry farms, friends were singing the praises of strawberry daiquiris. I found the strawberry slush so delicious that adding spirits seemed a waste. Soon I learned to love a liquid breakfast of fruit slush. At first I used apple juice for a

base, with a bit of orange juice for the tang. Into the blender with a cup of juice went one banana, fresh or frozen, and a handful of strawberries. If necessary, I add enough water to make the slush swirl. As new fruits ripen in the garden, I freeze the extra and experiment. I find a very little of grapefruit or papaya can be plenty. A bit of mint, lemon balm, or pineapple sage adds a nice touch. Try your own combinations. You can use almost any fruit this way with very little work. The drink is better than chocolate and much more nutritious. It is also a great way to start or stay on a diet or to use fruit without eating all the sugar of jams and pies.

**Fruit leather.** This year the plum tree outdid itself. We picked about two dozen plums every day from early May until the end of June. When I had frozen all I figured we would eat in the off season, I made fruit leather. It invoves blending a mix just a little thicker that the slush described above, and you can use any fruit. Try some after your first strawberry picking.

First cut up a blenderful of plums or other main fruit. Puree, then add one banana for sweetening, a few strawberries for color, half a cup of sugar if desired (plums can take on a certain bitterness once past their fresh stage), half a tablespoon of lemon juice, and half a teaspoon of cinnamon. Blend all this together and taste to see if you want to add anything else.

Then spray a large, edged cookie sheet or two 13" by 9" baking dishes with a non-stick coating or line with waxed paper. Pour in a thin layer of puree, up to 1/4 inches thick. Put it into your food dryer, if you have one, or the oven set on the lowest setting for 12 to 30 hours. Leave the door open two or three inches.

The puree dries to a thin, flexible sheet that you can cut into squares with knife or shears. Store in a tightly covered container. Thanks to the fruit roll-ups sold in the stores at a hefty price, even the neighbor kids gobble these up instead of candy. Experiment with whatever fruits you have in abundance. Add mint, lemon balm, or pineapple sage if you wish.

## THE FRUIT GROWERS CHOICES
The more you learn about growing fruit in Florida, the more you appreciate the incredible range of choices. Look on the next page for a chart of the main fruits and how and where they grow in different parts of the state.

Frost protection and, for some, chilling time in winter are deciding factors in your selections. Often you can grow borderline ones if you are ready for the challenge of protecting them in winter. And sometimes you lose the "safe" ones. After a deep freeze, our Rare Fruit Council International newsletter comes out with a black border, but we just try again.

## FRUITFUL CHOICES

| NAME | Type | Northern FL | Central FL | Southern FL | COMMENTS |
|---|---|---|---|---|---|
| apple | tree | best | fair | do not plant | Plant two kinds. Spray for disease. |
| annonas | tree | in tubs | in tubs | in ground | Deciduous. Delicious. |
| avocado | tree | in tubs | in tubs | in ground | Feed like citrus. |
| banana | tree | fair | good | best | Feed and water well. |
| Barbados cherry | tree | in tubs | protect | good | Acerola, high in vitamin C. |
| blackberry | shrub | good | good | good | Can be rampant. Mulch. Acid soil. |
| blueberry | shrub | best | good | poor | Plant 2 or more pollinating kinds. |
| calamondin orange | tree | in tubs | protect | good | Ripens October through January. |
| canistel | tree | in tubs | protect | good | Fruit like dry egg yolk. |
| carambola | tree | in tubs | protect | good | Protect from wind, also. |
| cherry of Rio Gr. | shrub | in tubs | protect | good | Dark red fruit, April through June. |
| Chinese chestnut | tree | best | good | do not plant | Deciduous trees, bear prickly burrs. |
| elderberry | shrub | good | good | good | Blooms & bears from frost to frost. |
| fig | shrub | good | good | good | Starts easily from cuttings. |
| grape | vine | good | good | good | Muscadines and Florida varieties. |
| grapefruit | tree | in tubs | protect | good | Pink or white, seedless available. |
| grumichama | shrub | in tubs | protect | good | Shrub with grapelike fruit. |
| guava | shrub | in tubs | protect | good | Landscape shrub or small tree. |
| jaboticaba | shrub | in tubs | protect | good | Delicious fruit right on wood. |
| jambolan | tree | do not plant | protect | good | Rampant tree, can take over. |
| jujube | tree | good | good | good | Small, reddish-brown fruit in fall. |
| kumquat | tree | protect | good | good | Hardy, salt-tolerant, 'Meiwa' sweet. |
| lemon | tree | in tubs | protect | good | Evergreen. Meyer is hardiest. |
| lime | tree | in tubs | protect | good | Key lime has good salt tolerance. |
| limequat | tree | in tubs | protect | good | Cross between lime and kumquat. |
| longan | tree | do not plant | in tubs | good | Easier to grow than lychee, hardier. |
| loquat | tree | good | good | good | Handsome tree, fruit like apricots. |
| lychee | tree | do not plant | in tubs | good | Protect from wind, mulch well. |
| macadamia nut | tree | in tubs | protect | good | Delicious nut from Australia. |
| mango | tree | poor | in tubs | good | Flavor varies. Buy grafted plants. |
| mulberry | tree | good | good | good | Delicious fresh, ripens Jan.-Feb. |
| natal plum | shrub | in tubs | protect | good | Easy ornamental. Fragrant flowers. |
| nectarine | tree | best | good | poor | Select grafted varieties. |
| orange | tree | protect | protect | good | Different varieties give long harvest. |
| papaya | tree | diff., use tubs | protect | good | Most need male and female plants. |
| passionfruit | vine | in tubs | protect | good | Lovely flowers, hand pollinate most. |
| pawpaw | tree | best | good | do not plant | Hard to establish. |
| peach | tree | good | good | good | Select varieties for N, C, or S. |
| pear | tree | good | good | good | Subject to fire blight. |
| pecan | tree | good | good | poor | Too big for small yard. Need two. |
| persimmon | tree | good | good | fair | Some Japanese cvs. not astringent. |
| pineapple | peren. | in tubs | protect | good | Pick just before fully ripe for flavor. |
| plantain | tree | in tubs | protect | good | Treat like bananas. Can eat green. |
| plum | tree | good | good | poor | Most like cold. Easy care. |
| pomegranate | shrub | best | good | fair | Fruits best after cold winter. |
| pommelo | tree | poor | protect | good | Large as grapefruit, more cold tender |
| prickly pear cactus | shrub | good | good | good | Tasty, eat fresh or in jams or juice. |
| raspberry | shrub | good | good | good | Only 'Dorma Red' and 'Mysore' cvs. |
| rhubarb | peren. | best | good | poor | Plant seeds, plants in fall as annuals. |
| rose apple | shrub | do not plant | in tubs | good | Attractive plant, new leaves red. |
| sapote | tree | poor | in tubs | good | Sapodilla, black and white kinds. |
| sea grape | shrub | do not plant | protect | good | Huge round leaves, seaside gardens. |
| strawberry | peren. | good, protect | good, protect | good | Grow as annual, pick Dec.-June. |
| Surinam cherry | shrub | in tubs | good | good | Attractive shrub, spicy fruit. |
| tangelo | tree | in tubs | protect | good | Cross betwn. tangerine and grapefrt. |
| tangerine | tree | in tubs | protect | good | Smaller, easy-to-peel fruit. |
| tree tomato | shrub | in tubs | protect | good | Large leaves, colorful fruit. |

At all times of year, there are outstanding ornamental plants throughout Florida. Drive a short way in any neighborhood, and you will see a colorful array of exotic palms, shrubs, and trees. Especially if you've prided yourself on knowing landscape plants in the North, you'll be eager to acquire information on these southern beauties. Even familiar plants like pin oak and sycamore behave differently in this climate. Leaves stay on past Thanksgiving. The oak leaves fall slowly all winter until a hard freeze brings all the rest down, or the new leaves push off the old ones in March.

A frustrating aspect of being new to Florida is not knowing the names and behaviors of all the strange new plants. And in the time you are getting to know them, it is likely that you will buy a few you later regret, or let less desirable types grow on your newly acquired property. Don't worry too much about this. Florida is a great place for starting over because shrubs often freeze back, sometimes with great advantage. They also come back from the roots if we let them, grow very quickly if we nurture them, and, in selected cases, die out if we don't.

If you drive more than a few miles in any direction, but especially north or south, you will find different plant species growing, and the same ones behaving differently. A short distance can make quite a difference in which plants can be grown. St. Petersburg has more tropical plants than does nearby Tampa. These get frozen less often and bloom earlier. The jacarandas bloom in April in St. Pete, but not until almost June in Tampa, if they survive at all.

Here is my list of recommended woody plants that you may see and want first. If you used to garden in a state farther north, and your new residence is in northern Florida, you will find trees that you already knew. In southern Florida, there will be few of these, but more of the wonderful tropical trees will grow and bloom without special protection. You'll soon learn the names and habits of those that do best in your neighborhood, as you visit nearby gardens and nurseries. Additional rare and unusual plants for your new garden will also become familiar as time goes on.

## SEMI-TROPICAL TREES

**Acacia** (*Acacia auriculiformis)* grows only in southern Florida, has flattened branchlets instead of leaves, and fountains of small yellow flowers. Except for hurricane or frost damage, it has few problems. You may find several other acacias at southern nurseries. All are cold tender and all have yellow flowers.

*Araucaria* **species** in southern Florida will probably be the Norfolk Island pine (A. *heterophylla*), unique in its dark green color and tiers of very horizontal branches. In central Florida you find another handsome araucaria that is the monkey puzzle tree, *A. araucana*. I could hardly wait to get one of these because my friend from Ireland loved them. There they are picturesque, very sparse trees, but here they are very dense, and as prickly as a tree can get. Mine died in the Christmas freeze of '89, and I did not replace it because the litter it made was painful to touch. Like many semi-tropical trees, this ones becomes hardier as it grows older. Many large monkey puzzle trees in my neighborhood survived the same freeze just fine.

**Bottlebrush trees** (*Callistemon* species) are small trees that grow 20 feet tall in central and southern Florida. They bloom in spring or summer with red-orange flowers that look just like their name. This is an excellent tree for color, as well as for luring bees to your yard to help with the pollination of vegetables and fruits. Large specimens do not transplant as well as smaller ones.

*Citrus* trees are as lovely as they are fruitful here. There are hardier kinds like kumquats that grow anywhere in the state. Some fruit in summer, some in fall, and some in winter. Check with your county agent for recommended varieties for your local climate, or buy from a trusted local nursery. Also see *Citrus* under fruit trees in chapter 8.

**Floss silk trees** (*Chorisia speciosa*) are planted to such spectacular effect at Cypress Gardens that you want to fill your sky with them.

But the few I see around us in Tampa bloom sparsely and skip whole years, even though we are at about the same latitude. Possibly this is because of salt water intrusion underground -- they have poor salt tolerance. The flowers are three to five inches wide, with five long petals in watercolor shades of off-white, rose, or lavender. Trees reach 40 or 50 feet in height and produce a silky seed floss used for stuffing pillows.

*Jacaranda acutifolia* grows 25 to 40 feet tall only in the central and southern counties, for it has little tolerance of frost. It has lilac-like but larger flowers that start as dark purple buds on a bare tree, then make a profuse cloud of lavender blooms, and finish with a few lavender flowers clear into August. Like other spectacularly flowering trees, the jacaranda drops petals and is otherwise somewhat messy, also short lived. The graceful, feathery leaves are deciduous and compound, and make light shade in summer. The silhouette is bare in winter.

**Oaks** (*Quercus species*) are the biggest trees in our neighborhood, spreading and producing acorns as in the North, but otherwise very different in leaf. Live oaks and myrtle oaks grow in every county of Florida. Laurel oaks and sand live oaks grow down to the everglades. Chestnut oaks and dwarf post oaks grow mostly in the southern counties, extending into the central region. Oaks are often planted in groups, though a single tree makes an excellent shade and specimen tree very quickly. They can grow five feet taller and wider every year. Most are evergreen, though the pin oaks have lovely winter color.

**Orchid tree** (*Bauhinia* species) is one of the showiest flowering trees in central and southern Florida. It grows to 20 or 25 feet with moderate speed and needs annual shaping for best umbrella form. Leaves are round but with twin lobes. Various kinds bloom at different seasons of the year with orchidlike flowers of white, lavender, or reddish purple, some up to six inches across.

**TREES WITH FRAGRANT FLOWERS**
- *Acacia*
- *Albizzia*
- *Citrus*
- *Magnolia*
- *Malus* species (apple)
- *Prunus* species (peach, plum)

**TREES WITH FRAGRANT LEAVES**
- *Myrica* species (Bayberry)
- *Eucalyptus*
- *Ficus* (fig)
- Pines

**TREES WITH SHOWY FLOWERS**
- *Acacia*
- *Albizzia*
- *Bauhinia* (orchid tree)
- *Cassia*
- *Citrus*
- *Cornus*
- *Chorisia* (floss silk)
- *Jacaranda*
- *Koelreuteria* (Golden Rain Tree)
- *Magnolia*
- *Tabebuia*

**SMALL TREES (under 25' tall, nice for small yards)**
- *Acacia*
- *Bauhinia* (orchid tree)
- *Callistemon* (bottlebrush)
- *Cercis* (redbud)
- *Citrus*
- *Cornus* (dogwood)
- *Eriobotrya* (loquat)
- *Ilex* (holly)
- *Pandanus* (screw pine)
- *Tabebuia*
- *Vitex* (chaste tree)

**LARGE SHRUBS, OVER 15'**
- Barbados cherry
- *Callistemon* (bottlebrush)
- *Camellia*
- *Coccoloba* (sea grape, in southern Florida)
- *Lagerstroemia* (crape myrtle
- *Ligustrum* (privet)
- Natal plum, some species
- Oleander
- *Pittosporum,* some cvs.
- *Podocarpus*

**MEDIUM SHRUBS 5' TO 10'**
- *Acalypha* (copper leaf)
- Azalea
- Burford holly
- Croton
- Dwarf natal plum
- *Gardenia*
- *Hibiscus*
- *Ixora*
- Japanese boxwood
- *Lantana*
- *Nandina*
- *Plumbago*
- *Raphiolepsis* (Indian hawthorn)
- Rose
- Roselle
- Surinam cherry

**SMALL SHRUBS 1' TO 2'**
- Harland boxwood
- Japanese holly
- Kurume azalea
- *Pyracantha* (dwarf)
- *Yaupon* (dwarf)
- *Yucca*
- *Zamia* (coontie)

The Hong Kong orchid tree is quite fragrant in bloom. Propagate by grafting or air layering. Salt tolerance is fair, drought tolerance good.

**Pines** (*Pinus* species) grow throughout Florida. The species differ from those of northern states, but are similar in needle and cone bearing, if not so much in overall shape. Traveling through northern Florida you may see vast forests of pine. Their trunks are the source of those long logs you see on trucks on the way to the sawmill.

In the northern and central part of the state you find pond, sand, longleaf, and loblolly pines. Slash pine grows from southern Florida as far north as Tampa. Pines are often planted in groups in Florida yards. They eventually tower above most of the other trees. The needles make excellent mulch. So do the heaps of pine cone chips the squirrels leave behind after savoring the edible pine nuts.

**Tabebuia.** Silver trumpet, pink trumpet, and others of the many *Tabebuia* species griw quickly into small trees, 25 to 40 ft. tall, with leaves in whorls of three to seven and trumpet-shaped flowers in clusters, followed by cylindrical pods. The hardiest, known as silver trumpet, tree of gold, or yellow poul, has an interesting irregular shape, silver-gray foliage, and bark with golden yellow blooms in late winter. Others bloom in shades of pink, rose, or white with colored veins, some with mild fragrance, all in late winter or early spring.

Some species have fair salt tolerance. All have excellent drought tolerance. They thrive in poor soil though they prefer it more fertile, and do well in sun or shade. They have few problems other than frost.

## PALMS

Palms in many sizes and kinds grow throughout Florida. They are variously hardy, and there is a wide selection on the coast and in the south. Northern Florida has only a handful of choices. David loves all palms, especially those with tall, unique shapes.

Most palms will grow in full sun to partial shade, are fairly salt tolerant, and are easily transplanted since they are shallowly rooted. All bear fruit, some of which is good for eating fresh or using for jelly. Everyone knows the date, for instance, which comes from date palms. Below Miami you find stands selling "coco frio," cold coconuts (from local palms) that are opened with a machete and served with a straw inserted for drinking the coconut milk.

Palms need watering during the dry months, feeding, and trimming of older fronds. Apply one pound of palm or regular fertilizer per inch of trunk diameter yearly, in February, June, and October in the south, in late winter and mid-summer in the north. Also apply half a pound of manganese and magnesium, up to five pounds yearly to minimize yellowing or frizzling of fronds.

## TALL PALMS

**Gru-gru** (*Acrocomia totai*). Central and southern Florida. 45 ft. tall. Black spines on its trunk can be vicious.

**King Palm** (*Archontophoenix* species). Uneven ringed trunk, graceful, young plants very cold tender.

King palm

Sabal palm

63

**Sabal or Cabbage Palm** (*Sabal palmetto*). Northern, central, and southern Florida. 60 ft. tall. This is the state tree and grows wild throughout Florida. It is extremely salt and cold tolerant, and has fragrant flowers.

**Canary Island Date Palm** (*Phoenix canariensis*). Northern, central, and southern Florida. 50 ft. tall. The trunk has a diamond pattern, like pineapple. Highly ornamental.

**Queen Palm** (*Arecastrum romanzoffianum*). Central and southern Florida. 40 ft. tall. Straight, ringed trunk. Needs full sun and is not very salt tolerant.

**Washington Palm** (*Washingtonia robusta*). Northern, central, and southern Florida. 60 ft. tall. Excellent for avenues but too large for small yards. Old fronds hang like a skirt. Needs full sun and has good salt tolerance.

## MIDSIZE PALMS

**Areca or Cane Palm** (*Chrysalidocarpus lutescens*). Central and southern Florida. Grows 20 feet tall in bamboolike clumps. Needs a frost-free climate and salt-free soil. This can be grown in tubs.

**Chinese Fan Palm** (*Livistona chinensis*). Central and southern Florida. 20 to 30 ft. tall. Grown for its large, fan-shaped, palmate leaves. The trunk is vaguely ringed. White flowers have an unpleasant odor.

**European Fan Palm** (*Chamaerops humilis*). Northern, central, and southern Florida. 10 to 15 ft. tall. This grows slowly in clumps and is good as a specimen or in small groups. It is the most cold-hardy palm.

**Fishtail or Tufted Palm** (*Caryota mitis, C. ureus*). Central and southern Florida. 20 to over 40 ft. tall. This grows quickly. Notched leaflets on fronds give it its name.

**Pindo or Jelly Palm** (*Butia capitata*). Northern, central, and southern Florida. 15 to 20 ft. tall. Grows slowly, has excellent salt tolerance and edible fruit, and gracefully curving, blue-green fronds. Needs room.

Sago palm

## SMALL PALMS

**Cycads.** These are not palms but ancient, leathery-leaved plants that resemble them. In the plant order, they are between ferns and pines. They grow very slowly, prefer shade, and have male and female flowers on separate plants. **Sago palm**, up to 6 ft. tall, is the shortest cycad and grows in all parts of the state. Others grow to 20 ft. tall. **Fern palm** grows only in the warmest parts of Florida.

**Coontie** (*Zamia floridana*). Northern, central, and southern Florida. Also a cycad, this plant has no aerial trunk but makes a low clump of fernlike fronds. It likes shade but tolerates sun and drought. Red scale can be a serious problem.

**Lady Palm** (*Rhapis* species). Northern, central, and southern Florida. Species range from five to 15 ft. tall. This is a moderate grower with poor salt tolerance. It grows in a clump, often with leaves to the ground. It prefers shade and is a good container plant.

**Date Palms** (*Phoenix* species). Northern, central, and southern Florida. Height ranges from dwarfs under 2 ft. to specimens 100 ft. tall. Date palms are hardy from Jacksonville south, but seldom ripen fruit here, though some I heard of in Clearwater produced six pounds one year. Pygmy date is useful in the landscape for its feathery foliage. It prefers shade and fertile soil. The Senegal date grows slowly in clumps, reaching 20 feet, and has good salt tolerance, but is hardy only in central and southern Florida. Neither of these bears quality fruit. The one that does, *Phoenix dactylifera*, is too big for most yards.

| **FRAGRANT SHRUBS** | **SHRUBS WITH SHOWY FLOWERS** | **SHRUBS FOR SHADE** |
|---|---|---|
| Crape myrtle | Abelia | Abelia |
| Gardenia | Azalea | Azalea |
| Jasmine | Bottlebrush | Boxwood |
| Oleander | Camellia | Camellia |
| Rose | Crape myrtle | Coontie |
| Sweet olive (*Osmanthus fragrans*) | Gardenia | Croton |
| Viburnum | Ixora | Gardenia |
|  | Indica hawthorn | Holly malphigia |
|  | Japanese privet | Ixora |
|  | Lantana | Japanese privet |
|  | Natal plum | Juniper |
|  | Nandina | Nandina |
|  | Oleander | Natal plum |
|  | Plumbago | Oleander |
|  | Poinsettia | Philodendron |
|  |  | Plumbago |

## HARDY TREES

Here are other trees familiar to former residents of states north of Florida:

**Cedars.** Here they are usually the southern red cedar (*Juniperus silicicola*) that ranges to lower central Florida or the white cedar (*Chamaecyparis thyrsoides*), also called false cypress, which grows in northern Florida.

**Dogwood** (*Cornus florida*) grows as far south as central Florida. It blooms variously every year, depending on the weather, and is often only a shadow of its northern counterpart. It is more reliable in northern Florida, but in central Florida, you can expect it to be outstanding only about one year in five. Other years they are mere reminders of other places, as they bloom sporadically throughout the winter instead of with one glorious show in March. Chances of successful growth are better in a shady site.

Dogwood or *Cornus* is plagued by the blight that affects it in other states. To help with disease resistance, prune off lower branches for better air circulation.

**Elms** here may be the Florida elm or the cork elm (*Ulmus floridiana* or *alata*). Both range mostly through the northern and upper central counties.

**Ginkgo** (*Ginkgo biloba*) is hardy from zone 10 northward. I have read that it grows well in Florida, but I haven't seen one here. I've seen them in California, so they must not mind heat.

**Holly** (*Ilex* species). Holly trees and shrubs are so lovely here that I am surprised to learn that we are their southern boundary. It takes a male and a female to have berries, but you can plant them both in the same hole and only we gardeners may notice that all the berries are on one side. Hollies are handsome for their shiny green foliage alone. Species vary from tiny to large leaved, spiny or smooth, mounded shrubs to tall trees.

**Linden** or basswood (*Tilia floridiana*) grows from the central to the northwest section of the state.

**Magnolia.** *Magnolia grandiflora* is a magnificent evergreen tree that has huge white flowers intermittently for much of the year, and large, leathery, dark green leaves. The leaves have a definite brown underside that makes the tree seem somber to some people. I see a few of the saucer magnolias blooming pink in December or January, and get that old spring feeling, but they do not grow large. They probably do better farther north. Some of my friends have star magnolias, but I have not seen them in bloom. These are shrubs here. The sweet bay or swamp bay tree (*Magnolia virginiana*) grows wild from northern to southern Florida, and blooms with lovely white flowers all summer.

**Maples** in our area (*Acer barbatum* or southern sugar maple) are colorful with small red leaves in late winter and red seed clusters in early spring. They do not grow large or wide, and we are probably near their southern limit.

**Mulberry** (*Morus rubra*) grows as far south as Tampa and has delicious fruits in early spring. Fruit drop can be a problem, however, especially where it stains a sidewalk or deck.

**Persimmon** (*Diospyros virginiana*) grows in northern and central Florida, but not much further south. Somewhat more heat tolerant are the many improved varieties of *D. kaki* with larger and better quality fruits than the native types. They are often grafted onto the wild rootstock. In the southernmost counties they do not fruit as well or grow as tall or wide, but in most of the state they make lovely, deliciously fruitful small trees.

**Redbud** (*Cercis canadensis*) grows in northern to central Florida, as it does in many northern states. But it is only a pleasant shadow of our northern memories, not nearly as showy, but nice. It is native to Florida, so I expect that every few miles to the north it improves in appearance. Big, heart-shaped leaves follow the linear sprays of rosy lavender flowers.

**Sourwood** (*Oxydendrum arboreum*) grows in northern Florida. Its other name is lily-of-the-valley tree for the flowers are strikingly similar. Leaves have a rich, dark red autumn color.

**Sycamore** (*Plantanus occidentalis*) has large, maple-like leaves and the trees may or not have a wonderful woodsy fragrance. Leaves turn brown about November and the trees are bare for about four months here. Tampa is their southern limit.

**Sweetgum** (*Liquidambar styraciflua*) grows all over Florida but does not have the lovely red autumn color here. Leaves seem to just dry up and fall off. It probably does better in northern Florida. It grows quickly with fair salt tolerance.

**Weeping willow** grows along streams and lakes throughout the state, but is not widely planted. I've seen a few. There are other weeping trees like the bottlebrush that are more decorative.

### IRRESISTABLE SHRUBS
**Azaleas** (*Rhododendron* species) bloom most abundantly and much more reliably at the same time as the flowering dogwood. They are beautiful together. They also have the same climate limit. More will grow in northern Florida, none in southern. They do best in full sun in northwestern Florida, in shade in the rest of their range. They require fertile, acid soil. Varieties range from dwarf azaleas to some that get ten feet tall and spread almost as wide. They begin blooming while very small. The yellow and orange-flowered types are missing here. Most of the prevailing pinks, whites, roses, and lavenders can be mixed lavishly without any clash of color, although they make more of an impact with at least three of a single color. Some will begin blooming in the fall and continue until their grand new show in March. Standard varieties are especially striking. None are salt tolerant. In Florida they seem more problem free than the ones I saw farther north.

**Camellia** (*Camellia japonica* and *C. sasanqua*). Camelias are hardy throughout Florida and are sometimes the only plant blooming after a frost. They thrive in partial shade and seem to grow taller, up to 15 or 20 feet, the further south you go. Leu Botanical Gardens in Orlando is a great place to see them.

**VINES FOR FLOWERS**
Allamanda
Bougainvillea
*Clerodendrum thomsoniae*
Coral vine
Cypress vine
Mandevilla
Moonflower
Morning glory
Passion flower
Thunbergia
Trumpet vine
Wisteria

**FRAGRANT VINES**
Japanese honeysuckle
Moonflower
Stephanotis

**VINES FOR SHADE**
Ivy
Honeysuckle
Smilax species
Virginia creeper
Philodendron
Pothos

Camellias grow slowly and like enriched, acid soil and partial shade. They should be mulched, especially in central and southern counties, and watered as needed. Buds will drop from dry plants. Exquisite flowers of white, red, and pink, sometimes variegated, bloom for a few weeks each from October to February, depending upon the variety. They have poor salt tolerance and some pest problems, and can die back in hot summers.

**Copper leaf** (*Acalypha wilkesiana*, ack-a-LYE-fa) does best in full sun and in the southern counties. It grows quickly and can get 15 feet tall. The large, coarse, evergreen leaves can be mottled copper, shades of red and purple, or green and yellow. Mine dies back in frosts almost every winter but always comes back and gets taller than the five-foot fence in no time. Flowers are catkins and tend to blend in with the colorful foliage. Copper leaf is salt tolerant behind the dunes and has few problems.

**Crape myrtles** (*Lagerstroemia* species) are shrubs or shrubby small trees that bloom all summer with pink, lavender, dark red, or white flowers. From a distance the clusters look like lilacs. That first summer I was so homesick that I resented the comparison, but now I appreciate the crape myrtles and even feel a little sorry for people who come to Florida every winter but never see this summer glory.

Crape myrtles grow quickly throughout Florida to about 20 feet tall. Species and cultivars vary in height. The leaf canopy is umbrella shaped, above bare trunks with attractively mottled bark. They like full sun but will take some shade. They are not salt tolerant. Their deciduous, small, oval leaves have some fall color that improves the farther north you live. There are varieties that are hardy as far north as Philadelphia. Some cultivars don't smell at all but some have a delightful lilac fragrance. They bloom on new wood, are easy to propagate from cuttings, and start to bloom when very small.

**Hibiscus** (*Hibiscus* species) can grow with moderate speed up to 15 feet tall in central and southern Florida. Farther north, grow it in large pots. For best bloom, provide full sun, plenty of water, and slightly acid soil. The flowers resemble hollyhocks but are larger and more singular. The color range includes all shades but blue and purple. They bloom for much of the year, blossoms appearing on new growth. The large leaves are evergreen, alternate, toothed, and dark green. A freeze will kill the plants to the ground in central Florida, but they usually come back. The related mallows die to the ground every winter as they did in Iowa. The similar looking, closely related rose of Sharon is hardy in northern Florida in shades of rose, white, blue, and lavender. Hibiscus species have few problems and root easily from cuttings, but are not salt tolerant.

**Gardenias** (*Gardenia* species) grow quickly in all of Florida and can get eight feet tall and equally wide, though mine stopped at five feet. They grow in full sun or high or light shade. Their shiny, evergreen foliage will have yellow markings if the soil is not acid enough; this is easy to correct with acidic or azalea fertilizer.

This was the first shrub I planted after moving to Florida. It is easy to grow here, but actually blooms for only a few weeks in the spring, and then seems to have as many old, faded flowers as new beauties. I wish now that I had put mine out of the limelight, but I do enjoy bringing the blooms indoors to float in a bowl and fill the room with fragrance.

**Nandina** (*Nandina domestica*) does best from central Florida north. It prefers clay soil and partial shade. It forms clumps of erect stems with large, fernlike leaves. These turn a lovely orange-red in the fall and contrast dramatically with terminal clusters of scarlet berries. I had seen nandina in the Tampa area, where it is not remarkable. When we made a trip north last fall, the nandina became more beautiful with every mile we traveled. Never judge a plant, especially in Florida, until you've seen it at its best.

**Oleander** (*Nerium oleander*) grows in full sun in all parts of Florida. Clusters of showy, single, five-petaled or double flowers bloom during much of the warm season in pink, red, white, or cream. Some varieties are fragrant. These shrubs can grow 15 to 20 feet tall, in time, but can be root- and top- pruned to stay smaller. All parts of the plant are toxic to humans. Oleander freezes to the ground at 26 degrees but will come back quickly from the roots. It has dark green, leathery, sword shaped evergreen leaves in whorls of three. The plants are poisonous to most insects but attract a strange oleander caterpillar that can defoliate them. Check plants closely. If yours are affected, dust them with *Bt*. Otherwise they are easy to grow, for they tolerate both salt and drought. Cuttings are not hard to root in moist sand.

**Pittosporum** (*Pittosporum tobira*) is an evergreen landscape plant widely used for hedges and foundation plantings all over the state. It grows rapidly in sun or shade with whorls of leathery, dark green or variegated evergreen leaves that are about three-inch-long ovals, squared off at the outer end. Pittosporum can grow to 15 feet and tries to cover our house, but takes well to trimming. Dwarf types are also available. The leaf clusters pruned off are attractive in bouquets. Where the plants do not have to be trimmed, they bloom with wonderfully fragrant terminal clusters of yellowish white flowers.

**Plumbago** (*Plumbago capensis*) was blooming when we arrived in Florida in June. It has such beautiful light blue flowers that I decided to buy one at once. Luckily, two were already growing in our backyard, one under the family room window where it attracts a constant flutter of butterflies.

Plumbago blooms best in full sun. It is hardy in central and southern counties, and will die back in a hard freeze. The foliage is evergreen, small, and graceful. The phlox-like flowers bloom all summer long and intermittently the rest of the year. Masses of it are used as groundcover in roadside and municipal plantings. I had never seen anything bloom for that many weeks per year before, but I've now grown used to that wonderful trait of Florida plants. The seeds of plumbago stick to clothing, so plant it where you need not brush against it.

There is also a red plumbago with terminal flower spikes. Both types are salt tolerant if planted well back of the dunes.

**Podocarpus** (*Podocarpus macrophyllus*, or Florida yew) is another popular evergreen that is used in landscapes all over the state. Like pittosporum, the foliage is useful and long-lasting in bouquets. The plants grow in shade to full sun with long, slender, blackish green foliage and edible blue berries. It is a fairly upright and graceful plant, but like the yew, can be trimmed to any size or shape. It can grow to 50 feet, but fortunately it is not that fast a grower. It is somewhat salt tolerant.

**Roses** (*Rosa* species) will grow in Florida as well or better than they do in the North, but they must be the types suited for this climate. Some of the old-fashioned roses like 'Louis Phillipe,' 'Baroness Henriette Snow,' 'Madame Lombard,' and 'Mrs. Dudley Cross,' most of the miniature roses, and some of the new landscaping roses will do well here. Hybrid teas and floribundas must be grafted onto special Florida rootstocks to do well in the central and southern parts of the state, so buy locally or from special catalogs for Florida.

There is an excellent rose garden at Cypress Gardens that shows what can be done with roses in Florida, and the new 'Bonica' pink landscape rose blooms there year round. At home, I have roses that have done as well as mine in Iowa, but have taken less care and coddling, especially regarding winter protection. And I've been to rose shows that prove you can have superlative success here.

Plant roses where they will have at least six hours of sunlight, preferably morning sun. Roses tend to grow taller here since they are never winterkilled, and need not be pruned back as severely. Prune dead wood any time, but do major pruning in January or February, even if plants are not dormant. I spray with water often to remove insects and disease spores, but early enough in the day for foliage to dry before nightfall. With mulch, fertilizer, and water as needed, I enjoy six or seven flushes of bloom a year. With more precise care and weekly spraying, much like in the North, one can grow show roses. Roses are moderately salt tolerant.

**Roselle** (*Hibiscus sabdariffa*), or Florida cranberry, is a plant I couldn't wait to grow. Started from seed in early spring, it makes a large shrub by late fall that is momentarily both beautiful and useful. Its petioles can be pink, green, or deep red, and most flowers are pink or red, though I had one that had yellow flowers with lime green calyces. It is the calyces that you pick for making jelly, tea, or juice. They are so pretty, I hate to say we don't much care for the taste that is supposed to be like cranberries but not as bitter. The plants die in the first breath of frost or else dry up and become ugly. Luckily

they are shallow rooted and easy to remove. They also self sow for me. Plant them where their unsightly decline won't matter.

**Sea grape** (*Coccoloba* species) is easy to recognize by its large, round, evergreen, often red-veined leaves. It is reliably hardy only in southern Florida, where it grows quickly to be a small, shrubby tree. My neighbors have to prune theirs drastically to keep it in a small yard.

This dramatic plant thrives in beach sand, loves full sun, and is completely salt tolerant. It can die to the ground in frosts in the central coastal area. It usually comes back, but never gets as large or as red as those in the warmer zone. The flowers are inconspicuous on foot-long racemes, but the purple grapes that ripen in summer are very good for jelly.

**Surinam cherry** (*Eugenia uniflora*) has shiny dark green evergreen foliage with bright red new growth. It reminds me of abelia. It does best in full sun in central and southern regions, grows quickly, but will stand heavy trimming, even as a clipped hedge. The flowers are small, white, and starry, and can completely cover the bush in the south, though they are not so conspicuous on mine. Edible berries look much like little pumpkins made of red or black jelly, and have a spicy taste and one or two large seeds in the center. Plants can bear several crops a year.

Surinam cherry is related to clove and guava. My first plant is about six feet tall but not productive. Another red planted next to a black are both bearing prolifically, and I have learned to love the red ones. The black ones are pretty but still too spicy for me. Wash and freeze any extras. The seeds pop out readily as they thaw. They propagate easily from cuttings or layerings, and come back after frost damage here in the Tampa area.

## VERSATILE VINES

Vines do so well in Florida that at first I found them threatening, or at the least, straggly, with coral vine covering huge trees. But I've learned now to appreciate nature's ways of combining plants. I have gone so far as to almost sacrifice a pine tree in my front yard as a support

for a moonflower that blooms at night for months on end, until a frost kills it back. Then it starts over from the roots and is blooming again by June at the latest.

Most Florida vines can also be used as ground covers, and some can be trained as shrubs. They are usually easy to propagate from cuttings. Use them for color, fruit production, screening, quick shade, and privacy. Learn which ones are rampant and which are easy to control. Train them as they grow and prune ruthlessly when necessary.

Deciduous vines like the Virginia creeper on my porch are ideal for giving shade in summer but letting in welcome winter sun, saving both heat and air conditioning costs.

These vines or vinelike shrubs grow well in Florida:

**Allamanda** (*Allamanda* species) will capture your eye and your heart with its four-inch, waxy, yellow flowers. A related form has strings of violet blue, orchidlike flowers. It is hardy in central and southern Florida, takes sun or partial shade, and grows quickly and easily to 10 feet in acid soil. Train as a sprawling shrub or give some support to use it as a vine. Its salt tolerance is fair, but wind and drought tolerance are good. It is poisonous, so warn children not to taste. It freezes at 32 degrees but usually comes back from the roots. It is common here in the Tampa area, where it blooms mostly in the summer. Further south it blooms nearly all year. In winter, keep a few cuttings rooting indoors in a glass of water, for frost insurance.

**Bougainvillea** (*Bougainvillea* species) is one of the showiest vines in central or southern Florida. It is an evergreen with sprawling, thorny canes, alternate, heart-shaped leaves, and tiny flowers that come in showy clusters of brightly colored bracts, usually in the rose, red, orange, or purple. It blooms during the cooler months, and some types change color as they age. The vines do best in full sun, grow quickly if well fed, die at 32 degrees but usually come back from the roots, and are fairly salt tolerant.

Prune when needed for shape, watching out for the thorns. Protect from caterpillars and keep the soil on the acid side, or the leaves will yellow.

Bougainvillea is lovely draped over a wall. A red one in Pompano Beach is skillfully and sparsely espaliered up to the top of a two story building. Another red one at Cypress Gardens grows as thickly as a waterfall and creates a breathtaking show. It is protected from frost to prevent dieback, which would thin the branches.

**Coral vine** (*Antigonon leptopus*, an-TIG-o-non) grows all over the state. Plant in full sun for best flowering. It blooms with strands of bright pink or white little heart-shaped flowers for months in late summer and fall. Use it to lure bees to your garden. Each flower spray ends in a curling tendril. In its native Mexico, it is called "chain of love" and the underground tubers are used for food. The foliage is light green, heart-shaped, coarse-textured, and prone to caterpillar chewing. It is best to cut the canes to the ground each winter.

**Clerodendrum** (*Clerodendrum thomsoniae*) is called bleeding heart, glory bower, or bag flower in Florida. It is nothing like the bleeding hearts we had up north, but it has its own subtle beauty with evergreen leaves, opposite and prominently veined, and white calyces or bags with bright red corollas extending beneath them. The white fades to pink and then purple, and clusters remain showy after the flowers drop for a long season of interest. It blooms in summer and fall, climbs by twining, is hardy all over the state, and dies back at 28 degrees but usually comes back. This is one of the few flowering vines that prefers partial shade. It has fair to low salt tolerance.

**Cypress vine and cardinal climber**, cousins of the morning glory (*Quamoclit* species, *Ipomoea quamoclit* and *I. angulata*, and *Mina*

*lobata*) grow wild in Florida. Also called **star glory**, these vines have multitudes of small white, red, pink, or lavender star-shaped flowers that stay open all day. They have either ferny or small, heart-shaped leaves, twine from ten to 20 feet, and bloom throughout the warm months. They thrive in dry soil and warm weather.

Cardinal climber is slightly larger than cypress vine in both flowers and foliage. It is usually listed in catalogs as *Ipomoea* x *multifida*. It has red flowers only. Plants come fairly true from seed, or can be started from cuttings.

**Virginia creeper** (*Parthenocissus qinquefolia*) looks and acts much the same in all of Florida as it does in states to the north. The whorls of five leaves are dark green, often with red markings. Some people consider this a rampant weed, but we let it curtain our screened porch because it does so gracefully with its little holdfasts like clinging hands. It comes down easily when it needs to be controlled. Annual vines like nasturtiums and moonflowers can intertwine with it.

**Jasmine**. See chapter 4 under ground covers.

**Honeysuckle**. See chapter 4 under ground covers.

**Mandevilla** (*Mandevilla splendens, M.* hybrids) has big flowers that look like hot pink allamandas. 'Alice du Pont' is one of several well-known, choice cultivars. This plant is sometimes listed as *Dipladenia*. Mandevilla is closely related to but vinier than allamanda, definitely more needful of support. It is hardy in central and southern Florida, with evergreen foliage. The vivid flowers are unusual in that they can double in size (three to six inches) after they open, and reach their richest color after several days. The plants like full sun and acid soil, and have slight salt tolerance.

**Morning glory** (*Ipomoea* species) is possible in Florida during the cooler months, but seldom flowers as prolifically as in the North. It is best sown in early spring, just after the danger of frost passes, or indoors two weeks earlier for a head start.

**Passion flowers** (*Passiflora* species) come in many and varied kinds in southern and central Florida. They are very sensitive to frost, and need protection, but mature plants often come back from the roots after a frost. The lovely purple flower we cultivated in a Pennsylvania greenhouse grows wild around us, but my efforts to tame it took several seasons.

The red passion flower, bold and beautiful with scarlet, recurved petals and rounded leaves with scalloped edges, looks so different from the delicate blue that it is hard to believe they are related, but they are.

There are a dozen or more others, with at least three, including the giant granadillas, that produce edible fruit. In fact, Hawaiian punch is largely passion fruit juice.

The giant granadillas and yellow passion-fruit do best in the south. Purple passion fruit will grow wherever it can be protected from frost. All the passion fruits need acid soil, trellising or other strong support, frequent light feedings, full sun, and pruning to keep them within bounds.

Passionflower plants freeze at 32 degrees, and some come back. I knew of some that came back every year even in Iowa, but mine have not come back here yet. They are easy to start from seed or cuttings, and can fruit in one year from cuttings.

**Thunbergia**, also called black-eyed susan vine (*Thunbergia alata*) is easy to grow from seed. The multitudes of funnel-shaped blooms may be cream, yellow, or orange. The ones with pale centers are not nearly as showy as the black-eyed ones, but seed may produce either. You can weed out the paler ones after they start to bloom, if you wish. The vines bloom all year except after a frost, and grow as much as 30 feet, no problem. For more control, grow them in a hanging basket. They have covered and concealed a section of chainlink fence at my house, and now threaten some shrubbery. I only planted seed once and cuttings another time, and I've had them ever since.

**Trumpet vine** (*Campsis grandiflora*) grows and looks much as it does in other states, with massive vines with coarse compound  leaves, and loads of large, tubular, red-orange flowers. Although a rampant grower, it can be grown on strong supports, like wisteria, and trimmed regularly for a spectacular appearance.

**Wisteria** (*Wisteria floribunda, W. sinensis*) grows here, but not nearly as rampantly as it did in states to the north. It blooms briefly, but makes a poor showing compared to what you remember. I planted one not long after arriving, but so far I wish I hadn't, but do not have the heart or the strength to tear it out.

## STARTING NEW WOODY PLANTS

Many trees, shrubs, and especially vines can be propagated easily from:

**-seedlings.** Look for some coming up around the base of the tree or start seeds yourself in pots.

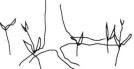

**-softwood or green tip cuttings.** Cut at a slant just below a node six to eight inches from the tip. Remove lower leaves and stick the stem into a pot or dishpan that has holes for drainage, and has been filled with vermiculite, perlite, sand, or some combination of these. Keep moist but not soggy. Most subtropical plants will root in two to six weeks.

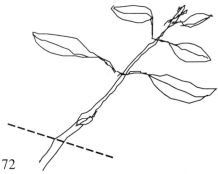

**-hardwood cuttings.** Try this if softwood cuttings fail. This is best done while plants are dormant or nearly so. Take six to 12 inches of pencil-size tip growth. Label. Stick into the rooting medium or ground so that only the tip or top one third is above ground. Keep moist but not soggy. Cuttings will usually root in two to several months.

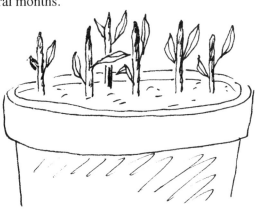

**-layering.** Bend down a piece of stem, and at the point where it touches the ground, cut or scrape away a small area of bark, down to the cambium layer. Hold it down to or under the ground with a rock, a hairpin-like wire, or such. Keep soil moist but not soggy. In one to six months, it will root where the bark was scraped. When roots are well developed, cut the rooted piece from the parent and transplant.

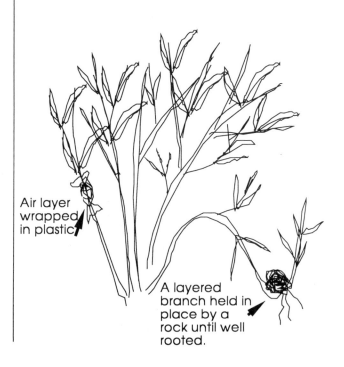

Air layer wrapped in plastic

A layered branch held in place by a rock until well rooted.

# CHAPTER TEN
## HOUSEPLANTS IN FLORIDA HOMES

Your houseplants, new or relocated, will celebrate your moving to Florida. Never again will they perish from living in a hot, dry, artificial atmosphere.

### WHO NEEDS HOUSEPLANTS IF YOU HAVE THE GREAT OUTDOORS?

I thought that I wouldn't need houseplants in Florida. The same plants that people pamper in states farther north will grow outdoors for most of the year here. I would no longer need indoor greenery to help me through long winter months of cabin fever. Nor would the plants need my indoor nurturing to survive the months of cold. Since it was both warm and rainy when we arrived, the few plants that made the trip seemed to deserve the same outdoor summer vacation that I would have given them had we stayed in the North.

But even in Iowa I always kept the contented houseplants inside in the summer on the theory that a happy plant, like a sleeping baby, should not be disturbed. Looking back, that may have been partly an excuse.

For with the move I discovered that I need green living plants indoors. Some people can get by with silk ones, but for me every room needs some echo of natural, green, growing outdoor life. And I'm not alone. Should you doubt the appeal of indoor plants, look through the photos in any decorating magazine and just try to find one without any houseplants in it. Most of those rooms look so great precisely because they have about three times more green or blooming plants than most of us use.

"People expect Florida to be lush and green and tropical, indoors as well as out," says one expert, Stormie Talmadge of Blue Lagoon Interior Foliage in Valrico. "Without plants, rooms seem sterile, bare, and artificial.

### PLANTS ARE EASY TO GET IN FLORIDA

Luckily, the boss from work sent the transplanted families each a dish garden, and some of the nurseries offered free plants with purchases.

"Plants are cheaper here," explains Ellen Skinner of The Plant Place in Plant City. "We aren't far from Apopka, Florida, which is the foliage capital of the world. They do grow houseplants in California and Texas, but there the many regulations add considerably to prices."

Some plants greatly treasured in northern climes, like lantana and Jerusalem cherry, show up as wildlings in our yards. Our choice of houseplants is large, and their need to readjust to the interior environment is small.

Growing plants indoors is easier here, for we have little drying heat and almost constant temperatures year-round in our houses. If plants need more light, we can rotate them to the lanai or outdoors under a tree until they form buds or green up, then bring them inside again to show off their blooms.

By the time I had established my mulch pickup routine (see chapter 4) I sometimes came upon discarded plants as well. One of my favorites is a variegated Benjamin fig. These are expensive to buy, and I had always read that they were difficult to grow, so I had passed them by even at garage sales. But when I found one in its pot, about eight inches tall and only slightly wilted, I brought it home and set it under the oak tree, my intensive care area.

It is now a full three feet tall and as lovely as lace. It sits by the front door (and is reflected in my computer screen in the study) for most of the year where it can enjoy fresh air and sunshine when the door is open. When its leaves begin to fall a few weeks after the air conditioning goes on for the summer, I move it back under the oak tree where it enjoys a growth spurt. It comes back indoors happily when the air conditioning goes off in September.

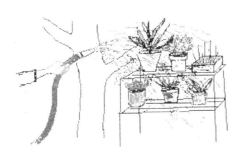

## BUGS AREN'T REALLY ALL THAT BAD

You hear much about the abundance of pests and diseases in Florida, and all that is partly true. But we have advantages, too. Some experts disagree, but many people have long thought that insects are more likely to attack plants that are under stress, and houseplants in Florida homes don't suffer the lack of humidity that is their worst enemy in heated houses.

The ghastly pair, mealy bugs and spider mites, will still attack on occasion. Try insecticidal soap. Talmadge uses two different kinds and switches back and forth so the insects won't develop an immunity to either. This soap is completely safe around people and pets, but bugs don't care for the taste.

If you have to use something stronger, systemic insecticides are safer because they go into the ground and up into the plant through the roots. Touching the leaves, even in a restaurant, won't hurt anyone. To use a strong spray like Omite or Pentac for spider mite or Malathion for mealy bugs, it is best to take the plants outdoors and treat them, to keep your house free of the poison. Often control takes two treatments, several days apart.

I haven't had to use any insecticide on any houseplant since we moved to Florida. At the most, I put it outside in the intensive care area where natural predators, wind, and frequent spraying with the hose tend to wash off both insects and disease spores.

## PLANTS STILL DO WILT AND DIE

This poorly understood fact causes more grief, guilt, and dissatisfaction in growing houseplants than is at all necessary. Once people realize and take this into consideration, they are free to enjoy their successes with most plants and the challenge of a few difficult ones.

For even in Florida, indoor plants often get less light and humidity, more smoke and cooking smells, or less help in pest control from

74

birds, little anole lizards, or beneficial insects than those growing outdoors. They are still vulnerable to too much or too little watering.

Many plants are naturally short lived or have cycles when they are not so attractive. Skinner says she finds dieffenbachia a short-term plant that soon tends to get long and leggy, so she does not use it often.

Outdoors, we let our plants go to seed or go dormant and don't give them another thought. We lose some, but the loss does not seem so traumatic. Indoors, those same plants are always in the spotlight. It is unrealistic to expect them to be perfect all the time.

Anyone who remembers northern winters also remembers how some houseplants began to show the strain as the months wore on. The same plants perked up and grew lush again if they got to spend summer outside.

Here in Florida we can rotate plants from the indoor spotlight to the porch or to a sheltered, shady part of the yard for rest and recuperation (R & R). Before long we accumulate lots of plants in pots, indoors and out. They all need protection from cold spells.

In northern Florida this means a few weeks of crowding all your potted plants indoors. Here in the central part of the state, I spread plastic on the porch and group containers just outside the sliding bedroom doors, where they are safe from all but the most drastic cold spell and I can enjoy seeing them. In southern Florida the periods of threateningly cold weather are even rarer, and are usually brief.

Indoor heat and, to a lesser extent, air conditioning, are hard on plants because they lower indoor humidity. But this situation is much less dramatic at any time in Florida, even northern Florida, than in northern winters. Added to that is the recuperative power of our warm and humid outdoor climate. It is so easy to put a lagging plant outside for a few weeks of refreshment.

The ideal would be to have two of every plant, one for the indoor spotlight and one for outdoor recovery, to be exchanged as needed. For people like me who would rather have variety than perfection, a passing parade of different plants is more enjoyable. Though I am still experimenting, my houseplants are more successful in my Florida home than they ever were up North.

I am now finding that some herbs that will not survive summer outdoors because of high heat and humidity will live indoors or on the porch until cooler weather arrives. Then they go back into the garden. Indoors or behind screens, they are protected from insects, and the constant shade makes the heat and humidity easier to bear.

## PLANTS NEED TO ADJUST TO NEW PLACES

Plant owners should be aware that drastic changes are hard on plants. In any new spot, the combination of light, humidity, temperature, and soil gives the plant an entirely new world. People cannot move into anyone else's house, or even a new house of their own, without some adaptations. Neither can plants. Some of their adaptations include dropping a few leaves or buds. Give a plant a few weeks before expecting it to resume normal growth.

It is also a good idea to put a new plant into isolation until you are sure there are no disease spores or insect eggs hiding in the crevices and waiting to spread to your other plants.

## DON'T LET THE TERM "DIFFICULT" DETER YOU

If you choose the right plant for the right place, the plant's adjustment will be minor and it will soon begin to thrive. If it does not, move it to other windows or rooms until you find the place where it is happiest.

If some of your plants die, it is not because you are a bad person who is sure to kill all plants. Just try another kind of plant or another place for the same kind. One lady I knew in Iowa had magnificent plants and was the only person I'd met in the North who could bring poinsettias back into bloom, but she couldn't grow philodendrons. Another told me that orchids were as easy as African violets, so I got some and found her right. I've killed many African violets since, but orchids keep on growing for me.

Success depends largely on the light, the house, and one's own tendency either to overdo the care of or to neglect plants. Overwatering is a common error that leads to root rot. Sometimes moving a plant to a room where you won't remember it so often improves its chances.

## MOST PEOPLE TEND TO OVERWATER AND OVERFEED

Professionals like Ellen Skinner and Stormie Talmadge work with plants in pots six inches wide or larger, and they almost never water more often than once a week. Many plants, especially in low-light situations, will go three or four weeks between waterings.

Talmadge says that the finger-to-the-soil test is the best way to tell if the soil is damp

## HOW TO HAVE FEWER PLANT PROBLEMS

* Pick the right plant for the right place. If your first pick fails, try again until you find plants that like your lifestyle and thrive in the light you can provide.

* Water only when needed. The smaller the pot and the brighter the light, the more often the soil will dry out. Provide drainage and never let plants sit in saucers of water for longer than 20 minutes.

* Fertilize only as needed. That will be more often during active growth, very little or not at all during short winter days.

* Watch for little white mealy bugs in the crotches. Spider mites are almost invisible, showing as a red dust on the undersides of the leaves. Their little webs don't show until the infestation is far along. If the leaves look pale or tarnished and the plant suddenly stops drinking as much water as it used to, treat for spider mites.

* An occasional shower, indoors or out, is a good pest prevention measure.that removes dust and perks up the plant.

* Young and rapidly growing plants need to be shifted to slightly larger pots as needed.

* Because they like humidity, plants tend to thrive in kitchens and bathrooms, all other things, like light, being equal.

* If a large plant starts to wilt more often or grow more slowly, it may be rootbound. Turn it out of the pot to check by holding the pot upside down and knocking it firmly on something solid. If the pot has more roots than soil, repot in a larger container or divide if possible. Be sure to leave 1/2 to 1 inch of pot above the soil line for watering.

enough or not. Some plants like to dry out between waterings, and others prefer their soil evenly moist all the time. Still others, like hibiscus and hoya, need quite a lot of water when they are in bloom and very little the rest of the time. All plants need more water when they are in active growth than they do when growth slows down for winter. That is not as sharp a contrast here, but the shorter days of winter make a difference, even when they are warm.

Skinner uses a moisture meter that she inserts into each pot. A dial on the top registers water needs. She waters or does not accordingly, and then pulls it out and sticks it in the next pot. These gadgets sell at stores like Wal-Mart and Home Depot for around $10. "I don't know how they work. There are no batteries or anything. I tell people it is magic," she says.

They are not supposed to last over six months, but she has used the same one all day three days a week for as long as two years. I bought one and it works well, but mostly I don't bother except for periodic checks. Something in the rod registers the moisture level on the meter.

**Interiorscaping.** People want plants indoors, lots of lush plants. And if they can't grow them themselves, businesses know the value of plants both for decoration and for morale in the workplace, and are more than glad to hire a professional plant service for their "interiorscape." Indoors as well as out, plants add charm, vitality, and individuality.

The rest of us enjoy growing our own houseplants. Some people succeed with everything from orchids to indoor trees. Skinner recommends pothos, bamboo palm, Chinese evergreen, and spathiphyllum as the most reliable and easy to grow, even in dark places.

Talmadge has some plants that have been in the same place for as long as four years. She says, "Often, when I do have to replace them, it is because they have grown too big."

## THE R & R AREA

The greatest blessing for houseplants in Florida is being able to be put outdoors for rest and recuperation occasionally or on a regular rotation basis. I have an area under a large oak adjacent to the rabbit pens where I am sure to be using the hose every day or so. The plants can survive with very little care during the rainy season and much less frequent watering than if they were in the sun. But plants in pots always need more watering than those in the ground.

### HANGING CONTAINERS
Plants in pots take more water than those in the ground, and plants in hanging containers take more yet, for evaporation is occurring on all sides. This is where water retaining gels (chapter 4) can make a great deal of difference. Hanging planters that normally would need watering as much as twice a day can go two days or more between waterings with gel in the soil.

Be sure that pots do not fall over (mine can get lost in the ferns). If necesary, repot them, including more sand in the mix to anchor them. Or drive a small metal stake into the ground and push a side pot hole down upon this.

Feed these plants the same way you would indoors, more often during the summer of active growth and frequent, leaching rains. Watch for insect damage or disease and prune as needed.

Don't be surprised if some plants escape the pots. I now have pothos, philodendron, Chinese evergreen, and several other houseplants growing as ground covers in that shady area. The Christmas freeze of '89 seemed to wipe them out, but they came back again from the roots.

## PORCH AND PATIO LANDSCAPING

Even more than indoor rooms, this transition room between outdoor and indoor living cries out for plants. What is more, it offers a fine haven for them. (See container growing in chapter 8.) Porches and screened-in patios offer additional advantages. Depending on location, they can get enough sunshine for most sunloving plants, enough shade for those that prefer shade, and in some cases, both!

In fact, a sunny, screened area is a lot like the shadecloth structures used by professionals to grow foliage plants for sale. The screening cuts the sun's intensity a bit, maybe ten percent, without putting the plants in the shade.

Porches will offer protection from wind. On the coast they can cut down on salt spray. If the porch or the entire pool area is screened, there will be no pests to do damage.

One of my neighbors, Ruth Feinberg, has a typical Florida room with the usual porch furniture for relaxing and a table and chairs for eating. But her porch also has unique decor: floor to ceiling, wall-to-wall potted plants. I find it enchanting, but it seems very labor intensive.

"No, it's easy," Ruth says. "I bring the hose in to water them. And the plants never freeze in the winter."

Our porch has a natural shelf all around the edge that holds windowbox type planters. A wicker plant stand in the corner holds a changing parade of accent plants, currently a rex begonia, another of the types that died for me in the North but thrives with little care here. Chains from the ceiling in the other corner hold either hanging baskets of plants or ripening bunches of bananas from our trees. Our indoor-outdoor carpeting survives drips well, but when I bring in the crowd of tender plants for their winter stay, a few weeks long, I put down a sheet of plastic first so I can water without worrying.

Don't let your plants give a feeling of encroaching upon your space. The population of plants on Ruth's porch does not. But it would only take a single hanging frond to make a few taps on my spouse's shoulder for him to send the plant outside or me for the pruning snips.

I like to keep some fragrant herbs like rosemary on the porch because it is such a handy place to rub them with my fingers as I pass or sit. And days when it is raining or dark, there they are, available for adding to the supper stew.

## BALCONY GARDENING
If your entire garden is only a balcony, you will want to use as much vertical and horizontal space as possible. Select shade or sun loving plants depending on which side your balcony faces. You can grow blooming plants like

verbena, vegetables like tomatoes, and fruits like kumquat on a balcony that gets six or more hours of sun a day. If yours gets less, grow houseplants like pothos, shade lovers like coleus, leafy vegetables like lettuce and spinach, or blooming plants in containers on casters that you move with the sun.

Wind can add some stress and cause more frequent watering, but it is amazing how much stress plants can survive, and how much they improve the area's ambiance. If your balcony is crowded with furniture and people, put the plants in corners or on shelves, or hang containers of them from the walls.

## PATIO AND DECK LANDSCAPING
Unscreened patios and decks should blend into the landscape as much as possible. Surrounding shrubs or vines in the yard beyond may help you achieve this. Here again, use plants and planters to hide undesirable views and frame the ones you treasure. Trellised vines are useful and beautiful, an easy way to add height to your plantings. In-ground planting areas within the patio or deck allow you to feature certain plants or trees and enjoy their shade as you sit.

Other planters with trees or shrubs can add to the feeling of privacy. Most of us don't mind if others can see us walking or working, but we'd prefer to be hidden while we sit and rest. Raised beds or large planters full of flowers can provide screening for this effect.

If your patio is sunny, it is an excellent place to grow the fruit trees and shrubs that are too cold sensitive to plant in the ground. They can provide shade, screening, flowers, fragrance, and the interest and taste of ripening fruit close at hand.

For colorful accents, nothing beats smaller containers of blooming plants on tables, steps, or in corners. Some of these, with petunias or pansies for winter, portulaca or vinca for summer, will have to come and go on a rotation basis. Others with long lasting plants like begonias or impatiens can stay for months before they need pruning back and R & R out of the limelight.

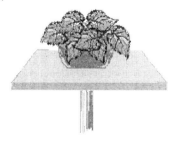

## MORE PATIO AND DECK TIPS

* Patio plantings are always in the spotlight. Avoid use of plants with messy parts: flowers and fruit that drop and make litter or stains, like mulberries, and flowers that look bad when they begin to wilt, like gardenias. If you use the patio mostly early in the day, plants that bloom only at night, like moonflowers and daturas, could be depressing. If you use it mostly in the late afternoon or evening, they are sensational.

One way to handle pots in sunny areas is to stack plants in pots on larger plants in pots. I do this with my fruit. On top of the soil in the huge pot that keeps the black sapote ready to run from frost, I set several gallon-size containers of other fruits all around the trunk. And if I come home with a raffle prize in a four-inch pot, I set that on the soil in one of the gallon pots. In full sun, all the plants get enough light, but this helps keep the roots shaded. I never lose or forget any of them, but feed and water them all at once. They grow fast, look great, and can be decorative if you add several pots of petunias or marigolds to bloom and cascade over the sides.

* Larger pots, more water-retaining material like peat, vermiculite, or gels in the soil, and terra cotta pots that keep roots cooler all help plants in pots in sunny areas. Be sure to check for water needs every day or two, at least.

* Plants that will survive in low light will grow even better in medium to slightly higher light areas.

* Remember to turn your plants counter-clockwise every few days if light from one side is stronger. This will keep them well rounded and prevent their leaning toward the light or having one bare side.

* Most houseplants that we grew in the North will not survive full Florida sun (Jerusalem cherry is the exception), but will thrive in partial shade.

Dracenas and crotons will have less color in deep shade than in partial sun. On the other hand, coleus and Joseph's coat will fade in full sun and have deeper color in partial shade. Most flowering and fruiting plants will do more of both with full sun.

## CLEVER CONTAINERS

Check your own attic or upper cupboards as well as garage sales for bean pots, crocks, buckets, tool boxes, baskets, wooden boxes, and wooden or ceramic planters that will hold plants and add to the decoration or mood as well.

I once had a cheese-making box but I never got around to making cheese. And at a farm auction an old wooden grocery box with old-fashioned labels on the side was thrown in with something else. Now I realize how perfect both would have been for plants, had they not gotten lost in one of the moves.

So now I look through my own and other people's "junk" with planting possibilities in mind. If a box has lots of character but no bottom, just put a plastic container inside.

One lady used her grown children's old wagon to hold a collection of potted plants. Rug tubes covered with adhesive paper will hold plants at various handy levels. An old birdcage will turn a pot into an interesting hanging planter.

You can buy or make wreaths full of sphagnum moss and soil mix to hold living herbs and succulents, then use them as wall decorations.

You can also buy or make "living wall" vertical units that hold a soil substitute in which all sorts of flowers, vegetables, or herbs grow. These columns, arches, or walls can be used on a rooftop, balcony, or even a boat deck.

## DESIGNER TIPS FOR YOUR TERRACE

Vince Sims, the Rebel Gardener of radio, TV, and books (see page 10), well known for his perfect handling of color in the garden, described some of his special techniques for me:

* Vince likes to match the kinds of pots to the mood of the landscape, using terra cotta with his own antique brick, large cement urns with lionshead handles with a formal house with pillars, glazed ceramic pots for a contemporary setting. But he adds that, while terra cotta pots may work best, it is quite possible to grow gorgeous plants in plastic pots or tin cans with drainage holes. You can then either transplant the plant or hide the pot or can in a more attractive container.

* Vince often repeats the color scheme of the surrounding gardens in the patio planters, for instance white petunias in the center of a ten-inch pot with hot pink ones around the edge when the beds are full of petunias of the same colors. A few months later he may try a completely different color combination like a multicolored English country garden theme.

* Vince uses up to one part of four of rotted cow manure in the potting mix for flowering annuals, adds Osmocote (TM) as needed, and does some liquid feeding as well. His landscapes are marvels of color.

* He combines various plants in the same large container. For instance he will use foliage plants like the arching Kentia palm in the center or back of a container, with annuals like salvia. Or he'll combine African iris (*Dietes* species) with cascading verbena for a bold contrast of texture and height.

Vince and other Florida landscape designers truly enjoy the Florida climate and find inspiration in the wonderful, sometimes exotic plants, with their striking textures and colors, that thrive in it. And so will you, as you adjust to gardening in Florida.

## RESESOURCES:
*Mail Order Suppliers*

**Blake's Nursery**, Route 2, Box 971, Madison, FL 32340

**Burpee**, 300 Park Avenue, Warminster, PA 18974

**Chestnut Hill Nursery, Inc.**, Route 1, Box 341, Alachua, FL 32615

**Clyde Robin Seed Co.** (wildflowers), 25670 Nickel Place, Hayward, CA 94545

**Daylily Discounters**, Route 2, Box 24, Alachua, FL 32615

**Edible Landscaping**, P.O. Box 77, Afton, VA 22920. Catalog $1.

**The Fig Tree Nursery**, P.O. Box 124, Gulf Hammock, FL 32639

**Florida Keys Native Nursery, Inc.**, US 1 and Mile Marker 89, Tavernier, FL 33070.

**Gardener's Supply Company**, 128 Intervale Road, Burlington, VT 05401

**Great Outdoors Publishing** (Florida books), 4747 28th Street North, St. Petersburg, Florida 33714

**Gurney's Seed & Nursery Co.**, 110 Capital Street, Yankton, South Dakota 57079

**Harris Seeds**, 60 Saginaw Drive, P.O. Box 22960, Rochester, NY 14692

**H. G. Hastings**, P.O. Box 115535, Atlanta, GA 30310

**Hearthstone House**, 1600 Hilltop Rd., Xenia, OH 45385. Slate garden ornaments.

**J. L. Hudson**, P.O. Box 1058, Redwood City, CA 94064. A vast array.

**Johnny's Selected Seeds** (short-season), Foss Hill Road, Albion, ME 04910

**Kinsman Company** (tools), River Road, Point Pleasant, PA 18950

**Kilgore Seed Company**, 1400 West First Street, Sanford, FL 32771

**Leonard** (A.M.), Inc. (tools), 6665 Spiker Road, P.O. Box 815, Piqua, Ohio 45356.

**Liberty Seed Co., Inc.**, 128 Ist Drive SE, Box 806, New Philadelphia, OH 44663

**Logee's Greenhouses** (tropicals), 55 North Street, Danielson, CT 06239

**Ann Mann's Orchids**, 9045 Ron-Den lane, Windermere, FL 34786

**Mellinger's, Inc.**, 2310 W. South Range, North Lima OH, 44452-9731

**Mickler's Floridiana, Inc.** (books), 181 W. Broadway, PO Box 1450, Oviedo, FL 32765

**Necessary Organics**, One Nature's Way, New Castle, Virginia 24127-0305

**North Walton Nursery**, Box 1143, DeFuniak Springs, FL 32433

**Orgel's Orchids**, 18950 SW136th St., Box K-6, Miami, FL 33196

**Park Seed**, Cokesbury Road, Greenwood, SC 29647-0001

**Pinetree Garden Seeds**, (small packets, mixes), Box 300, New Gloucester, ME 04260

**Roses of Yesterday and Today**, 802 Brown's Valley Road, Watsonville, CA 95076

**Seeds Blum**, Idaho City Stage, Boise, ID 83706

**Seeds of Change**, P.O. Box 15700, Santa Fe, NM, 87506

**Shepherd's Garden Seeds**, 6116 Highway 9, Felton, CA 95018

**Smith & Hawken,** 25 Corte Madera, Mill Valley, CA 94941

**Steve Ray's Bamboo Gardens**, 909 South 79th Place, Birmingham, AL 35206

**Thompson & Morgan, Inc.**, Box 1308, Jackson, NJ 08527

**Tomato Growers Supply Company,** P.O. Box 2237, Fort Myers, Florida 33902

**Twilley Seed Co.**, Inc., P.O. Box 65, Trevose, PA 19053-0065

**TyTy Orchard and Vinyard**, Box 130, TyTy, GA 31794 (for orders 1-800-532-3902)

**Van Bourgondien & Sons**, Inc., Box A, Route 109, Babylon, NY 11702

**Wayside Gardens**, Hodges, SC, 29695

**We-Du Nurseries**, Route 5, Box 724-BB Marion, NC 28752

**Willhite Seed Company**, (seeds for South), P.O. Box 23, Poolville, TX 76487

**Woodlanders**, 1128 Colleton Ave., Aiken, SC 29801

80

# GARDENS TO VISIT

If you are interested in visiting Florida gardens to see how to deal with conditions similar to yours, there are opportunities in all parts of the state.

Check first with your local Cooperative Extension Service, usually listed under county numbers in the phone book. You can also call the University of Florida in Gainesville (904-392-1781, Extension Office) for the number.

Many local extension offices have display gardens that are both inspiration and explanation. Visit them often to see how plants change and seasons vary. Also watch for notices on the garden page of your newspaper for classes, garden tours, special displays, sales, and other events. Consider joining a local garden club or plant society of your special interest. Ask about them at the reference desk of your library.

Listed below, alphabetized by location, are just some of the many gardens open to the public. Phone first for current visiting hours and prices, which change often. On your visits, you may be able to watch plants develop through the seasons, attend classes, see demonstrations, use libraries, browse through the horticultural bookstore or giftshop, or question experts. Some facilities combine special plantings with other attractions that non-gardening members of the family can enjoy. Some offer annual passes at reduced prices.

**Bonita Springs:**
   **Everglades Wonder Gardens,** Old U.S. 41 South, Bonita Springs, FL 33923. 813-992-2591. A Florida wilderness with animals.

**Coconut Creek:**
   **Butterfly World,** Tradewinds Park South, 3600 W. Sample Road, Coconut Creek, FL 33073. 305-977-4400. Rain forest plants, tropical habitat for butterflies, botanical and flower gardens, and plant shop.

**Cypress Gardens:**
   **Cypress Gardens,** P.O. Box 1, Cypress Gardens, FL 33880. 813-324-2111. A theme park with wide walks and boat rides through

botanic and rose gardens. New butterfly conservatory. Annual chrysanthemum festival in mid-November.

**Dania (west of Ft. Lauderdale):**
   **Flamingo Tropical Gardens,** 3750 Flamingo Road, Davie/Ft. Lauderdale, FL 33330. 305-473-2955. Heliconias, bromeliads, magnificent trees, train ride through fruit orchards. Plants for sale at gift shop.

**Fort Myers:**
   **Thomas Edison Home,** 2350 McGregor Boulevard, Fort Myers, FL 33901. 813-334-3614. Many plants collected and used by Edison as well as orchids, trees, and a bougainvillea hedge cover 13 acres of a waterfront park featuring Edison's Florida home.

   **ECHO, Inc. (Educational Concerns for Hunger Organization).** 1730 Durrance Road, North Fort Myers, FL 33917. 904-543-3246. Stop for informative scheduled tours, 10 am several mornings a week, or to visit their plant nursery.

**Gainesville:**
   **Kanapaha Botanical Gardens,** 465 S.W. 63 Boulevard, Gainesville, FL 32608. 904-372-4981. Call for schedule. Herb, butterfly, rock, bamboo, cycad, hummingbird, spring flower, sunken, wildfflower, and other gardens.

**Hawthorne:**
**Marjorie Kinnan Rawlings State Historic Site.** Route 3, Box 92, Hawthorne, FL 32640. 904-466-3672. Call for schedule. Site of *Cross Creek*. Home, grove, and vegetable garden of the author of *The Yearling*.

**Hialeah:**
**Hialeah Park,** East Fourth Avenue and 25th St., Hialeah, FL. 305-887-4347. Tropical gardens bloom along with the racetrack season from mid-January through mid-March.

**Homestead:**
**Redlands Fruit and Spice Park,** 24801 Southwest 187th Ave., Homestead, FL 33030. 305-247-5727. A large collection of rare and economically important trees, edible landscaping choices, and poisonous plants.

**Key West:**
**Ernest Hemingway Home,** 907 White-head Street, Key West, FL 33040. 305-294-1575. Trees and plants from much of the Carribean region.

**Peggy Mills Garden,** 700 Simonton Street, Key West, Fl 33040. 305-294-2661. Now a hotel, grounds have a very good collection of orchids and tropical plants.

**Lake Wales:**
**Bok Tower Gardens,** Lake Wales, FL 33859. 813-676-1408. Mountain Lake Sanctuary, designed by Frederick Law Olmstead. Camellias, azaleas, native Florida plants, and ferns are featured on 50 acres. Daily carillon recitals.

**Miami:**
**Fairchild Tropical Garden,** 10901 Old Cutler Road, Miami, FL 33156. 305-667-1651. One of the largest and most famous botanical gardens in the country with important collections of palms, bromeliads, ferns, tropical flowering trees, and orchids.

**Parrot and Jungle Gardens,** 11000 SW 57 Avenue, Miami, FL 33156. 305-666-8834. 11 miles south of central Miami, tropical gardens featuring a petting zoo and playground.

**Vizcaya Museum and Gardens,** 3251 S. Miami Avenue, Miami, FL 33129. 305-579-2708. 70-room Italian palace with ten acres of formal gardens and gondola rides.

**Orlando:**
**Leu Botanical Gardens,** 1730 N. Forest Ave., Orlando, FL 32803. 407-246-2620. Camellias and orchids. Rose garden, flower gardens, native plant garden, streamside garden, bookshop, and more. Classes and lectures.

**Ormond Beach:**
**Ormond Memorial Art Musem Gardens,** 78 East Granada Blvd., Ormond Beach, FL. 904-677-1857. Tropical gardens with gazebo, nature trail, fishpond and fountains near museum.

**Palatka:**
**Ravine State Gardens.** P.O. Box 1096, Palatka, FL 32178. 904-329-3721. Dramatic plantings of azalea and camellia along terraced ravine gardens date from the 1930's.

**Palm Coast:**
**Washington Oaks State Gardens,** 6400 N. Ocean Blvd., Palm Coast, FL 32137. 904-445-3161. 389-acre park with rose gardens, ponds, and ornamental gardens, on the intracoastal waterway.

**Port Orange:**
**Sugar Mill Gardens,** Herbert Street, Port Orange, FL. 904-767-1735. 12 acres of botanical gardens and flowering trees surround ruins of an old English sugar mill.

**Sarasota:**
**Marie Selby Botanical Gardens,** 811 S. Palm Ave., Sarasota, FL 34236. 813-366-5730. World orchid center, tropical plants, bromeliads. Conserrvatory and display gardens. Frequent classes and special exhibits. Book and plant shops. Library open to members.

**St. Augustine:**

Gallegos House, 21 St. George St., features a walled garden. Salcedo House, 42 St. George St., has a Spanish garden. The Gonzales-Alvarez House, 14 St. Francis Street, the oldest house in the U.S., offers herb gardens and plants of the period, including grapes and figs. These historic sites are supervised by the Historic St. Augustine Preservation Board, P.O. Box 1987, St. Augustine, FL 32085. 904-825-6830.

**St. Petersburg:**

Sunken Gardens, 1825 4th Street N., St. Petersburg, FL 33704. 813-896-3186. More than 7,000 species of plants on seven acres: natives plus colorful flowers, trees, and fruits from tropical countries. Rainforest and xeriscape plants are featured.

**Tampa:**

Busch Gardens, 3000 Busch Boulevard, Tampa, FL 33674. 813-971-8282. Fine display plantings around theme park and brewery; landscaping for wild animals in extensive zoo areas.

Eureka Springs Botanical Gardens, 6400 Eureka Springs Road, Tampa, FL, 33620. 813-744-5536. This 31 acre Hillsborough County Park has many rare plants, labels, a helpful staff, a greenhouse, a picnic area, and about a mile of trail. Admission is free.

U. of S. Florida Botanical Gardens, S.W. corner of Tampa campus, Alumni and Pine Drives, Tampa, FL 33620. For information call 813-974-2235.

**Tallahassee:**

Alfred B. Maclay Gardens State Park, 3540 Thomasville Road, Tallahassee Fl. 904-487-4556. Has the finest collection of azaleas and camellias in the South and over 300 acres of trees. Best in spring.

**West Palm Beach:**

Mount's Botanical Garden, 531 North Military Trail, West Palm Beach, FL 33415. Great display and herb gardens plus gardener education, rare fruit, test gardens, and much more.

# INDEX

## *ABOUT THE AUTHOR*

Monica Moran Brandies lives near Tampa and enjoys growing all kinds of ornamental and edible plants in her half-acre yard. She has been gardening and writing about her successes and mistakes since college days at the Pennsylvania School of Horticulture (now part of Temple University). She studied floral design under Bill Hixson in her greenhouse days and has been learning about growing plants in Florida since moving there in 1987. She is the author of *Sprouts and Saplings* (Strawberry Hill Press, *Xeriscaping for Florida Homes* (Great Outdoors Publishing Co.), and Herbs and Spices for Florida Gardens (B.B. Mackey Books). Her articles appear in many garden magazines and she writes a popular newspaper column for Central Florida. She contributed to *Better Homes' New Garden Book* and *Step-by-Step Landscaping,* and to Ortho's book, *All About Trees,* and its forthcoming herb book. She is the coauthor of *A Cutting Garden for Florida* (B. B. Mackey Books), which stresses growing and using floral material in Florida, and is also geared to newcomers to Florida.

# BOOKS FOR GARDENERS

## HERBS AND SPICES FOR FLORIDA GARDENS, by Monica Moran Brandies.

* Monica's NEW book brings you dozens of herbs and spices. She shows what to grow and how to do it, and how to use your herbal bounty for scent, flavor, color, health, and beauty. Florida's climate let's us have exotic spices in addition to the traditional herbs. You can grow plants like bay laurel, vanilla, lemongrass, neem, curry tree, and ginger that are left out of northern-focused books. The book is 5 x 8 1/2 inches, over 220 pages long, illustrated and indexed, with an extensive plant-by-plant directory.
ISBN 0-9616338-6-7                   $15.50

## A CUTTING GARDEN FOR FLORIDA, SECOND EDITION, by Betty Mackey and Monica Brandies

This concise and inspiring classic tells how to grow flowers for bouquets in Florida's unique climate. It covers the garden calender and the ins and outs of growing annual, biennial, and perennial flowers. Here are clear instructions on improving Florida soil and conditioning flowers, plus tips on making fresh and dried arrangements. Illustrated and indexed, printed on recycled paper, 96 pages measuring 7 by 8 1/2 inches.  **ISBN 0-9616338-2-4      $8.95**

## XERISCAPING FOR FLORIDA HOMES, by Monica Moran Brandies

"Use this book as a resource to create the most hospitable, colorful, and efficient garden possible. The environment will benefit and so will you," says Monica in her award-winning book on waterwise Florida landscaping and gardening with the best plants and techniques. 181 pages, 81/2 x 11 inches, illustrated and indexed.
ISBN 0-8200-0411-1          $18.00 (list $18.95)

## FLORIDA GARDENING: THE NEWCOMER'S SURVIVAL MANUAL, by Monica Moran Brandies

Florida has a garden rulebook all its own! Here's how to prepare for the move, make a landscape plan, use great looking exotic plants, decide which Florida grass type to plant, reduce labor and watering, turn Florida sand into rich soil, select appropriate plants for the site, grow fruits and vegetables, and use designer tips to decorate patios and poolsides with plants. Illustrated and indexed, 8 1/2 x 11 inches, 86 pages, printed on recycled paper. Anyone relocating to Florida needs this frustration-saving guide!
ISBN 0-9616338-3-2          $9.95

**GARDEN NOTES THROUGH THE YEARS,** designed by Betty Mackey. Here is an inexpensive, attractive, sensible journal for keeping notes on any four years of gardening activities. Each page spread lets you see notes for the week for all four years, so you can compare them at a glance. Illustrated with classic etchings and line drawings. 8 1/2 by 11 inches, 118 pages, sturdy covers. Cover personalized with any name on request.  **ISBN 0-9616338-4-0      $10.95**

---

## B.B. Mackey Books, P.O. Box 475, Wayne, PA 19087

Please send ___ copies of **Herbs and Spices for Florida Gardens @ 15.50**

Please send ___ copies of **A Cutting Garden for Florida @ $8.95**

Please send ___ copies of **Xeriscaping for Florida Homes @ $18.00 (list $18.95)**

Please send ___ copies of **Florida Gardening: The Newcomer's Survival Manual @ $9.95**

Please send ___ copies of **Garden Notes Through the Years @ 10.95**

Personalize **Garden Notes** with the name:_____

Free shipping and handling for **any 2 or more** books to the same address. **For one book, add $1.25 for shipping and handling.** Pennsylvania residents only, add 6% state sales tax.

SEND TO: Name_____

Street_____

City_____ State_____ Zip_____

Please include payment. Satisfaction guaranteed or return for refund. For more information call Betty Mackey (610-971-9409). Also available from Great Outdoors Publishing (813-525-6609, call for terms).